In Defence of Life

Pragmatic Proposals for a Planet in Distress

In Defence of Life

Pragmatic Proposals for a Planet in Distress

Julian Day Rose

EARTH

BOOKS

Winchester, UK
Washington, USA

First published by Earth Books, 2013
Earth Books is an imprint of John Hunt Publishing Ltd., Laurel House, Station Approach,
Alresford, Hants, SO24 9JH, UK
office1@jhpbooks.net
www.johnhuntpublishing.com
www.earth-books.net

For distributor details and how to order please visit the 'Ordering' section on our website.

ISBN: 978 1 78279 257 4

A CIP catalogue record for this book is available from the British Library.

Design: Lee Nash

Printed and bound by CPI Group (UK) Ltd, Croydon, CR0 4YY

We operate a distinctive and ethical publishing philosophy in all areas of our business, from our global network of authors to production and worldwide distribution.

CONTENTS

"To the unseen spirits that help us on our way."

With Thanks:
To Aidan Rankin for his thoughtful and insightful support in editing the text.

Foreword

Hitherto, the human evolution has been driven mostly by survival rather than enlightenment. Physical survival necessitates progressive cognitive abilities. The probabilities and dangers in nature have pushed our passion towards understanding our own existence in relation to the universe. Civilisation as we know it presupposes a degree of enlightenment involving the moral and spiritual practice.

The theory of Yin and Yang used in explaining the multitude of changes in our universe since the Big Bang has been the guiding principle of Dao (Tao) throughout Chinese civilisation. Together with the concept of Qi (vital forces or energy) the metaphysical thought in ancient Chinese philosophy is now finding parallels in the new physics of super-symmetry and quantum fields. With this new synergised energy between East and West, the human enlightenment is about to make the next qualitative leap. The emergence of the next Axial Age is upon us.

The latest thinking on the biologically based universe suggests a possibility of a universal quantum consciousness. This collective consciousness may provide us with a new view in understanding our existence. Scientists are now more than ever feeling somewhat insecure as their experimental evidence based methodology is being turned on its head. Both Einstein and Niels Bohr have publicly expressed that anxiety. There are many multi-dimensional realities that cannot be detected by human senses alone. Seeing is no longer believing.

How are we coping with this on the social and environmental level at the present moment in the history of human evolution? I'm afraid we are not doing that very well. Our environment is being depleted and polluted by the relentless quest for economic growth, the reckless use of technology and the material greed of the consumer culture. Indeed, in this process we have sacrificed the noble human values of enlightened and harmonious existence. Let's hope that the next stage of civilisation will be built upon human enlightenment and that the call to 'take control of our destinies', so strongly expressed in Julian Rose's illuminating text, is adhered to by an increasing proportion of humanity. To achieve that, we must now change the way we live 'in defence of life'. Can we afford not to?

Our total health, involving our body, heart and mind, is the link in the cycle of existence that holistically connects everything within this universe. I suggest that the change should begin with each of us cultivating our moral and spiritual self. A harmonious heart and an inspired mind in all of us will help to create a healthy society. Act now to ensure a brighter future for our children and the survival of the Earth.

Professor Man Fong Mei
The Chinese Medical Institute and Register, CMIR, London
Professor Man Fong Mei
梅万方教授

AcuMedic and Associated Organisations
亚美迪医药集团

Chairman, Chinese Medical Institute and Register (CMIR)
伦敦中医学院院长 与英国中医注册学会会 长

Chairman, Chinese Medical Council (CMC)
英国中医管理委员会主席

Chairman, China-UK Consortium for Medical Integration, Research and Collaboration (CUC)
英中医药合作联盟主席

Executive Chairman, Advisory Committee for Working, World
Federation of Chinese Medicine Societies (WFCMS)
世界中医药联合会工作咨 询委员会主席

Chairman, Mei Group PLC
梅氏集团董事长
99 -105 Camden High Street, London, NW1 7JN, UK
Tel.: +44 (0) 207 388 6704
Fax: +44 (0) 207 387 8081
www.acumedic.com
<http://www.acumedic.com/feedback>

Please click on the logo to visit our website:
AcuMedic
<http://www.acumedic.com/>CMIR
<http://www. cmir.org.uk/>CMC
<http://www.cmc-uk.org/>CUC
<http://www.cuconsortium.org/>chinalife
<http://www.chinalifeweb.com/>

Professor Mei expresses his view on health, medicine and other
East-West intellectual issues in his MFM E-Letter, his MFM Blog
and on Twitter.

Subscribe to the MFM E-Letter at no cost at:
http://www.acumedic.com/email-updates/mfm_e-letter/

Follow Professor Mei on Twitter @Prof.Mei

Read the MFM Blog at:
http://mfm.acumedic.com
<http://mfm.acumedic.com/>

Introduction

I experience life as an essentially joyous gift which is severely jolted each time some sanitising force tries to block its celebratory instinct. I recognise that 'normal' is the word used to describe this sanitised condition and that most of society 'suffers', in consequence, from normality. But I believe that this state is not inevitable and is the result of a largely superficial and superimposed process of indoctrination that blocks us from discovering something far more potent and joyous in ourselves and in the life we aspire to build around us.

The essays you are about to read, are mostly recent writings and have sprung to life as a result of their author having come face to face with such 'blocks' and having to find the appropriate actions to try and overcome them. The source of inspiration for these actions mostly spring from the heart. From this you will gather that the writings in this book are informed predominantly from this region, and are less descriptive than poetic in nature.

While much of the last three decades have found me immersed in a culture of food, farming, political activism and community regeneration, I have never felt these to be limited to professional *metiers*, more springboards on the voyage of Life.

We live in a compartmentalised culture that stifles holistic awareness and represses the true spirit of humanity. We see clearly how decades of monocultural political dogma produces a similarly impoverished culture. In the same way, a large number of monocultural farms engenders an impoverished landscape, starved of diversity. The food produced on these farms is poor or mediocre in character, intended for impersonal and unquestioning mass consumption. Food, landscape and culture are intimately related, overlapping entities. Dealing with them as disconnected, impersonal objects is to separate body from soul and to renounce beauty in favour of a commitment to the 'economics of efficiency'.

My decision to convert the family farm to an organic system, back in 1975, was informed by a strong desire to nurture into life a number of mostly small scale 'living' enterprises that would constitute a viable economy and a creative working environment. Amongst the influential factors shaping this aspiration was E F Schumacher's book *Small is Beautiful*, with its deep wisdom, practical grounding and sense of the 'human scale' that inspired many members of my generation.

However, my field of interest also included the arts and particularly the new genre of experimental theatre that was gaining prominence in the 1960s and '70s. In 1968/9 I attended The Royal Academy of Dramatic Art in London with the intention of gaining experience as an actor and stage manager. But after a short spell working in traditional repertory theatre, I went in search of something that would satisfy a more deeply rooted need.

Fortunately, I was invited to join a well-established experimental theatre company whose founders were deeply committed to evolving a fresh art of the theatre, and whose ethos chimed with my own aspirations. The work incorporated a creative exploration of the underlying connectivity between voice, movement, music and the written word.

The jump from dramatic art to the art/science of organic agriculture was rendered somewhat less extreme due to the fact that Lady Eve Balfour's Soil Association had already developed an understanding of the need to work 'with' rather than 'against' nature, which could be translated from theory into practice with relative ease. The development of the environmentally friendly food production system that became known as organic farming was now demonstrably possible.

This relatively sensitive approach exposed the destructive forces at work within the chemically dependent regime of industrial farming that still dominates most of the world's post-industrial agriculture to this day. It also highlighted the interdependence of soil, plants, animals and humans. When well maintained, this symbiotic relationship constitutes a dynamic cycle of health.

I was excited to recognise an underlying principle at work here that bridged the gap between my experimental theatre work and the practicalities of growing food. Both were based on cyclical relationships rather than discrete, disconnected entities. This recognition enabled me to jump enthusiastically into the development of my organic farming enterprises at Hardwick.

Although much of the writing in this anthology goes well beyond the constraints of a land based way of life, it is the reality of being 'well earthed' that has given me the confidence and foresight to offer an often fierce critique of the political and corporate exploitation of our planet and its peoples.

This same grounding has enabled me to put forward practical solutions to problems that threaten to overwhelm us and that should outlive the superficial and essentially false premises upon which much of our present society is constructed.

I hope you will draw sustenance by joining with me on the sometimes turbulent ride through the pages that follow!

I

Breaking the Cult of Passivity

If it's true that 'All the World's a Stage', then our role is to create a change of scene and a new play.

Our role in this play is to join with other members of the cast in unearthing and exposing the deeper significance of events being played out on the global stage and helping to unveil a new way forward, beyond the cult of passivity holding back the emancipation of a large portion of humanity.

The global stage currently more resembles a battlefield than a cultural arena framed by a proscenium arch. War zones today are defined as 'theatres' and the real action is supposed to be happening there: amongst the killing fields. Meanwhile our halls of artistic expression are mostly treated as useful distractions from the 'real business'.

It is more than time to reverse this ill contrived distortion and to rewrite the script.

'The script' is a key part of any drama and provides the actor with his or her frame of reference, without which the action soon loses its way. So we who contribute as writers seek to establish contact with our audience via our scripts. Our hope is that those of us who engage with these words will also become actors (those who take action) rather than merely passive spectators. If our aim is to help inspire a revolution, this response from our readers, our 'audience', becomes critical indeed.

In the theatre, the word 'revolution' may be used to describe the turning of a revolving stage, a device used to depict a scenic evolution of events. However, a revolution is more usually associated with an event or series of events altering the socio-economic course of history, breaking the hold of the status quo and leading society (or even humanity) in a new direction.

When we use the word 'revolution' in these pages, we mean all these things, but also a change in our individual and collective consciousness as human beings, in particular in the way we view our relationship with the natural world. By realigning ourselves with nature, we also change our relationships with each other and rediscover our inner selves.

For such a revolution to succeed on both the world stage and the theatre's stage, a strong script and perceptive direction become necessities. But from the outset, recognition must also be given to the abilities and skills of the actors. There must be the desire to share the creative task of bringing the drama to its full potential and not simply using the players as pawns in a process of achieving a desired result. Therefore, bringing the drama of revolution to its full potential is a shared creative task.

Writers, directors and actors have clearly defined roles – but what of the audience?

In the traditional theatre, the audience witness the drama from a removed and largely passive position. We in the audience are 'absorbers' of the action but are not participants in its outcome. Revolving the stage into the outside world, we see that this represents an exact mirror of the state of society. A large proportion of our society is essentially onlookers and, as in the theatre, share the *frisson* but do not deem it fitting to become involved in the creative process.

We talk excitedly, or gloomily, about the various scenes being played out on the world stage. We react in horror when someone whom we thought of as 'the good guy' turns out to be 'the bad guy'. We berate those 'in control' for stealing our money and poisoning our food. We despise their myopic attempts to run the show, resulting as it does in so much self-indulgence and outright destruction. We curse them for so brazenly exploiting our mute passivity. In short, we put our own hypocrisy centre stage. We, the audience, singularly fail to realise the part our passivity plays in shaping the global drama.

It is surely this process more than anything else that is the single greatest obstacle to change.

So long as 'watchers' fail to become 'participants' no major shift in the status quo can take place.

Yet you are reading this on the pages of a book which seeks to bring about change, so can I assume that somewhere inside, you are yearning to take action. And if not, then why not?

As the writer of the script, I need you to fill this role so as to give meaning to my words. Without your creative response to my creative input, these words will not achieve their true resonance. Of course, if you deem this to be a poor script, a poor response is only to be expected.

However, if perhaps you are already an actor (activist), then you will know what I am talking about and you will know that unless the audience (the public) is somehow motivated to get beyond receiving your endeavours as simply 'a nice performance', your labours will fall on stony ground. Thus the issue of 'the audience' finding a completely new role within the unfolding of the drama becomes of paramount importance in creating the conditions for radical change: change from the roots upwards.

The traditional theatre separates the auditorium from the stage – often with an orchestra pit in between. The seated spectator is given the role of onlooker, while the actor has the role of action maker. Put another way: members of the audience are cast as 'the many', who applaud 'the few'. The few are presented on a raised platform and, in turn, bow to those who applaud them. Thus the theatre in this conventional form apes the social status quo with its human-made divisions of 'poverty' and 'privilege', 'the people' and 'the elite', 'obeisance' and 'arrogance': the split society which still to this day holds humanity back from achieving some form of shared forward dynamic.

So the necessity is to forge a new role for 'the audience' which changes this hopelessly static position. If the audience is treated as a reserve of energy instead of a mere receptacle, its members and the actors alike share the common goal of bringing the drama to its full realisation. 'Full realisation' could be described as that which produces a transforming effect on all present.

This approach challenges the convenient assumption that the best we can expect from all who tread the boards of the world stage is that some will achieve notoriety while the rest provide the applause ... or the boos. The touch paper for revolution in consciousness is lit when a critical mass of 'we the people' are motivated to change our role from passive onlooker to active change maker.

Historically, the problem with revolution is that it usually only succeeds in eliciting a reversal of roles within the framework of the society in which it takes place: those on the bottom rise up, while those on the top sink down. But the division itself continues as before, just in a reversed order. In theatrical terms, the audience members become the actors and the actors become the audience, but otherwise nothing is changed. The architecture of society and the theatre remains essentially confrontational. Thus the so called 'revolution' fails to bring about the profound change we are looking for. Instead it merely turns the previous social and economic relationships on their heads.

Throughout much of the 1970s, I worked with an experimental theatre company, led by director Harvey Grossmann and poet Ruth Mandel, which set in motion a new phase in the evolution of the theatre, both humanly and architecturally. The writer, director and actor are viewed (and view themselves) as collaborators and colleagues, rather than occupants of demarcated and often adversarial roles. Therefore, they recognise that they are participating together so as to engage in a shared aspiration of a higher nature.

The working climate of such an innovative experimental theatre is exploratory: to give expression to the underlying vibratory pattern which drives, and is common to, poetry, movement, music and the spoken word. It's an exploration which is open to all ages, having the effect of stimulating and awakening untapped human resources and re-engaging the underlying connections between areas which are typically treated as separate disciplines. In other words, the theatre becomes a holistic experience.

During the course of this experimental theatre work it became possible to discern ways of channelling creative energies into the active pursuit of an awakened, revitalised and redirected aspiration to challenge all that stands behind the deeply destructive materialistic ideologies that dominate our planet today.

It is significant, perhaps, that parallel intuitions and discoveries took place during the 1950s and '60s in the physical sciences. In Quantum theory, for example, even the most minute of sub atomic particles, on inspection under a powerful microscope, are found to be in a constant state of flux. Their appearance fluctuates between a speck, a wave and what Quantum physicist Niels Bohr once called 'a dance'. A theatre form built upon the dynamics of movement thus crosses over with the 'dance' observed by the quantum explorers. These patterns are mirrored and replicated throughout nature, providing insights into the ways in which human society might be organised and the forms human cultures can take. They represent the true or 'natural' rhythms of our humanity, into which we can now begin to re-tune.

Such developments demonstrate the great value that could be gained from bringing into much closer proximity 'activists' 'artists' (and creative scientists, for that matter) in pursuit of the radical change or revolution as we have defined it above. Artists and activists are probably misleading delineations anyway, since the aspirations of each have much in common. Nevertheless, thousands of performing artists contribute next to nothing towards efforts to prevent the auctioning off of our planet by the purveyors of darkness and ignorance, *Avidya* in Hindu philosophy. Yet there are millions who still feel drawn to live performances of the dramatic arts, so this is clearly a highly appropriate medium in which to be introduced to a new way of engaging in an active process of change.

Almost daily, we hear a new story about the horrors being enacted by those who manipulate the levers of the top-down control system and their seeming determination to inflict untold damage to our lives and to our planet. Yet, even as these horrors are enacted, millions of new children are born onto our planet and millions of young people are passing through their adolescent lives in the hope of finding some creative outlet for their youthful energies. The fact that this hope is stymied again and again by a tunnel vision, money-obsessed status quo, means that most never find their way into avenues that could channel their positive energies into helping to bring about a process of creative change.

Education (Latin: 'e-ducare' 'to lead out from') is transformed from a potentially exciting process of discovery into an exam factory designed to fulfil the demands of a terminally sick consumer society. While mainstream media outlets, that should be the cornerstone of awareness raising, instead pour out titillating superficial stories, meaningless game show 'entertainment' and 'news' which is carefully edited to avoid any information of real value. All this is part of a carefully orchestrated dumbing down exercise that has a mesmerising or drug-like effect on those watching and listening. What is being absorbed is largely 'disinformation' put out by a state and corporate mass propaganda machine. It should come with a health warning. Better still – dispense with your television set and thereby remove one more toxic ingredient from your household.

Exposing the dominant system's desperate attempts to keep the lid on human potential for creative change makes big demands on all of us so engaged. The need is to counterbalance this work with a process that leads to a deepening of our lives and an expansion of our vision of what ingredients to pour into the mould of the new society which it is our prerogative to bring to birth.

We can only gain insight into what to do about the multiple problems thrown up by a civilisation moving into the advanced phases of collapse by drawing ever deeper upon our inherent (some would say God-given) artistic and creative abilities: here lies a fountain of life whose capacity for positive change is infinite.

By reviving the role of the creative arts as a key tool for activism, we can catalyse that largely pacified divine energy flow and pour it into the task of ousting the life-paralysing regime that exerts political and psychological power over us, putting in its place something of greater social and spiritual worth.

Deep down we are all 'artists'. In the new born child is contained the seed of all creative potential. It is just that (for most) at some point in the evolution from young child to grown adult, the vital spark is downgraded and its potency neutered. The genius in humanity is subverted into conformity to the banal.

Yet hidden within all of us, the child genius remains present and the open canvas of innocence retains its potential. This life line is always present, however dimmed, even if we fail to recognise it. It is the child in us which expresses the instinctive, spontaneous desire *to participate* in the drama of life. In this, the child is the original Actor. Why should this instinct be cut off? Is it not our lot to give expression to the genius we inherited?

Only by breaking through the cult of passivity can 'we the people' shift the momentum of society away from its present fatal trajectory into full alignment with the life-affirming forces that are the Divine's great gift to humanity.

2

Unmasking the Real Terrorists

For so long we in the UK have been asked to believe the governmental proposition that combating 'the threat of terrorism' is a national priority for which the taxes extracted from our hard-earned incomes are indispensable . We have repeatedly been told that it is for 'our national security' that the US/UK and other European accomplices send their military into Middle Eastern Countries to topple heads of state, destroy infrastructure and subject tens of thousands of men, women and children to an untimely and hideous death from bombs and bullets. We were, in the case of Libya, even told by serious looking politicians in grey suits, that the invasion was a 'humanitarian intervention' and that the death and destruction which accompanied it was a necessary part of 'protecting civilians' against the edicts of their own ruler.

All the while, here at home, a steady build-up of high-tech surveillance equipment has been tracking us as we go about our daily business. CCTV cameras, emails, text messages, telephone conversations, cash machines, credit cards, satellite images, all these and more can now be accessed in the supposed interests of curtailing potential home based 'terrorist' activity. So much so, that it appears we are now all viewed as potential threats to the nation. Ever since 9/11, we have been paying out of our own pockets to be protected from mythical 'evil empires', demagogic tyrants and crazed despots, only to find that we are also now conjoined with them on the suspect list.

Yet, in spite of this discovery, hardly a British whimper has been registered in response. The majority of the population of our island appear to be saying "Take my money, I trust you to know what to do with it Mr Blair, Brown and Cameron. We know you care more about people than about money and power. We accept that you have only humanitarian considerations at heart and would not allow the prospect of cheap oil, minerals and foreign military bases to cloud your vision. We are grateful for the protection you accord us. We know that there may be nasty terrorists plotting to overthrow our country at this very time. This is a democratic country; we are civil people. After all, it was we who spread democracy all over the world in the first place wasn't it? How ungrateful those people are who now want to seek revenge on us!"

Such a reaction, should it stand up to reasonable scrutiny, bears testimony to one of the most problematic features of British society: its refusal to look in the eye its own long record of conquest, pillage and murder. Indeed this record is often callously portrayed as a great crusade of empire building. There remains a lingering, stubborn determination, to see such British barbarism as nothing other than the valid expression of an unquestioned racial superiority. The moral presumption whispered around the coffee tables of the British bourgeoisie for decades, has been that other less 'developed' countries should be helped to 'come up to our standards'. Whereas the reality was not even one of patronising morality, it was grand conquest and all that entails.

The reason why the British ruling class is still operational today is because of the largely passive acquiescence of a society ordered on the principle of 'haves' and 'have-nots' or 'lesser' and 'superior'. This suggests an unspoken moral assumption in favour of class divisions which are falsely equated with a simplified, populist version of Darwinism: the idea of 'the survival of the fittest'. In this way, one part of society accepts – albeit grudgingly – its subjugation by the other, based not on the attributes of wisdom and example but on a hierarchy of wealth and power.

By uncritically accepting such subjugation within one's own

society, the basis is laid for the condoning of foreign invasions and the same process of subjugation being applied to the victims of these invasions. In this way war becomes rationalised and accepted as a natural part of preserving the status quo. It is just a short step from here to accepting the unimpeded imposition of a 'big brother' totalitarian style control system. The type so prophetically foretold by George Orwell and, in a softer yet more insidious form, by Aldous Huxley in the first half of the twentieth century.

So long as the majority of citizens hold onto a sense of nationalistic pride when their country sets off to invade a foreign country – then they will be perfectly conditioned to have this same 'war state' imposed upon them. And this is where we are today in Britain. The same symptoms are of course strongly borne out in the USA and beyond, but I am concentrating on Britain here, not least because of the role which Britain still plays in master-minding the strategies behind such conquests. This is based on the considerable reserves of British experience in perfecting the controlling techniques necessary to keep the subjugated from rising up in defiance, techniques often viewed as models by newer or emerging powers.

If 'the people' were able and willing to recognise the heinous levels of impoverishment and slavery that the British ruling classes imposed upon their vanquished populations – we would at least have a chance of understanding the origins of the present crisis. If it was also recognised that the divisive repercussions of these actions are still being played out in Africa, the Indian subcontinent and beyond, then we would be in a position to put the groundwork in place for a genuine resistance to the establishment of the 'surveillance society' which is closing in upon us today.

As the ominous beat of war drums herald preparations for yet another invasion (this time the Persian Gulf) so do our political figureheads once again straighten their ties, stiffen their necks and reel-off the well-rehearsed war-speak agenda: in this case the 'inevitability' of having to take action if Tehran refuses to bow to the will of the West.

We seem to be living in thrall to a doctrine of perpetual war. This has a cruel, crushing and conditioning effect on the human psyche, breeding suspicion and fear, where what is called for is clarity, understanding and courage. The clique of countries at the forefront of the sabre rattling are those least willing to examine their own failings. Their historical records have been carefully written to disguise the bloody truth behind their own acts of terrorism, conquest and empire building. History is only allowed into the national curriculum if it somehow manages to gloss over the horrors carried out in the name of aid, education and honour.

The insupportable misadventures of modern day invasions of the Balkans, Iraq, Afghanistan, Libya and by proxy Syria are still being defended as rightful incursions by those who swallow the political rhetoric of the 'war against terror'. And even when the motives for the invasion are proved false, other alibis are invented to try and give a veneer of authenticity to the true motives for invasion.

With the tacit permission of the electorate, a whole raft of infrastructural elements of the repressive control state have been put in place in the name of protecting against a 'terrorism' which is little more than a grand illusion, carefully constructed to pave the way for the imposition of a lock-down on any elements unwilling to conform to the creeping strictures imposed from above. The police have already gained access to technologies so sophisticated that they are able to 'monitor' the exact where-abouts of any individual they wish to track in real time. Doubtless they will soon be applying for the right to fly CCTV equipped 'drones' over homes and businesses anywhere in the country.

We have moved far beyond the territory which constitutes 'infringements of civil liberties' and are now in the domain of what amounts to authoritarian rule or dictatorship masquerading as democracy. The national and international war criminals who stand as unflinching totems of this 'democratic dictatorship' and its 'war on terror' are merely mirror images of the evil they claim to be fighting. They have yet to be seriously challenged.

What was once called "The Peace Movement" appears to have largely gone into hiding and is incapable of raising a coherent voice in opposition to the drum beat of war. Left-leaning citizens and Greens, who might be expected to raise their voices, have so compartmentalised their interests as to appear oblivious to the breadth of the social engineering going on in front of their noses. What should have incited a people's revolution has instead been assiduously allowed to establish itself as the necessary price to be paid for keeping the Taliban as far East of the English Channel as possible – the Taliban, who not so many years ago were nurtured by the CIA as part of the Cold War machine.

Those who have so cynically contrived to put in place the building blocks of the modern surveillance state are still in positions of power and have often accumulated immense personal wealth. They have been able to do so because the citizens of 'Great Britain' have for far too long averted their eyes from misdeeds both past and present. Collectively, we have continued to brush the accumulated bloodstained dust under the colonial carpet. For too many of us, this has proved easier than honestly and rationally facing up to the unpalatable reality that stands behind the events which made the small island of Britain one of the wealthiest nations on this planet.

So the real terrorists walk amongst us. They hold high office in our lauded institutions and come together to hold a missile to the head of any nation which does not conform to the agenda required of it. They will apparently go to any lengths to maintain the power structures to which they are accustomed and to acquire the oil and mineral wealth deemed necessary to maintain and expand these structures. Britain and the USA stand shoulder to shoulder in their role as purveyors of this terror regime, scheming up the most effective way of upholding this twenty-first century version of colonial conquest. They have, between them, engineered the domination of vast tracts of this planet under the guise of what is euphemistically named 'the special relationship'. It is a relationship forged out of the collaborative art of conquest, suppression and theft and sold to the world as the means of ' maintaining global stability.'

Only when a critical mass wake up to this reality and see it for what it is without taking the evasive action of denial, will we finally be in a position to turn the tide and set in motion a whole new agenda for the future of mankind.

There is no time to waste. We are either going to be complicit in the launching of a third world war of disastrous proportions or we are going to become the masters of our destinies and genuine peace makers – throwing off the chains of serfdom in the process. As masters of our destinies, we will become purveyors of a new kind of justice for those whom we once enslaved and whose wealth helped bestow the title 'Great Britain' upon this island once known simply as Britain. Britain still can be 'Great' but only when we Britons have set aside the false vanities and misappro-priated pride that has been the historical passport for conquest and suppression. Freed from this karmic burden, Great Britain can instead come to the aid of those countries still struggling to rise above the perverse forces of repression, aggression and greed for which we, wittingly or unwittingly, established such a tragic template.

3

The Organic Chimera

Back in 1975, when I first started converting my farm to organic agriculture, there were virtually no formalised standards for production and no rule book. There were just a few people committed to weaning their land off agrichemicals, improving soil fertility and supporting good animal health through regular crop rotations and through the sensible applications of farmyard manure. It was about taking a caring attitude to the overall welfare of our farms and trying to engender a wide bio-diversity of species within the farmland habitat.

We were not overly concerned about financial profit, but were interested in making an adequate return on our investments and in the quality, flavour and freshness of the foods we produced. We were perhaps more mindful than most of the words of Soil Association founder, Eve Balfour, that 'organic' food should be mostly unrefined and distributed and consumed locally, in its optimum condition.

I decided to develop my farm at Hardwick, in the Chiltern Hills of South Oxfordshire, on a mixed farming model, utilising a wide number of grasses and herbs in the lays and retaining all the 'never ploughed' permanent pasture that cover the chalk hills and sweep along the Thames-side meadows. My view was that the dairy cows, sheep and beef cattle that I purchased to graze these meadows would produce subtle, fine flavoured milk and meat and would be kept healthy through ingesting their particular choice of medicinal herbs and hedgerow leaves, at will.

I was not disappointed. The cattle thrived and the crops grew free from disease. We were able to start a local unpasteurised milk and cream round that was much appreciated by local country people. When, in 1989, the government tried to ban raw milk, I led a 'Campaign for Real Milk' and we beat them off.

As I continued to build up the enterprises on the farm, so the milk round offered the sale opportunity for a wider choice of fresh and local organic produce grown and raised on the farm: free range eggs, butter, pork, beef and table poultry. And in 1986 Hardwick's smoked bacon won the first ever Soil Association Food Award.

The organic farming movement was being born and there was a sense of excitement in the air. We were proving that the wisdom of old was alive and well: one could contribute to the long-term sustainability of the land while producing robust, wholesome foods in sufficient volumes to satisfy local needs and produce a modest economic return. At that stage there was no premium, no mass production and no supermarket sales. We were an embryonic movement which shared much in common with the fast disappearing traditional mixed family farms whose standard practice included rotational farming and minimal applications of agrichemicals.

What 'organic food' and its localised market were in those days bears little resemblance to the industry that it is today. 'Organics' have become a commercial enterprise that is heavily and centrally policed, has a compendium of regulations and is 'big business' on a global scale. In fact, much of the 'organic' produce shipped in from around the world and across the UK today carries no sense of connection with its geography or its farmers. It is as anonymous as the majority of conventional chemically produced foods, as dull in flavour and as lacking in nutritional vitality. What's more, most organic produce belongs in the category of 'high food miles' heavy ecological footprint produce, exceeding the 3,000 kilometre average shopping basket once identified as the UK norm. Due to the need to carry a lot of information, it is also responsible for an excessive level of packaging – most of which is not biodegradable.

All this is a far cry from what might be considered a respon-sible and sustainable form of 'greening' the agricultural sector; and a far cry from the original aspiration that organic food should stand for 'unrefined, fresh, local and seasonal'. Today one can even purchase 'organic' certified ultra-heat treated (UHT) homogenised milk in supermarkets, a product that bears no resemblance to real milk at all. However, there just might have been some compensation for this consumer oriented form of 'green' indulgence had the level of UK land converted to organic farming methods shown substantial increases throughout this time. But this is not the case. Official statistics reveal that there has been a negligible level of land converted to organic status over the past 20 years. It has remained pretty much static at around 3 to 4 per cent of UK farmed land throughout this time.

So apart from the resilience of a small body of local producers who have helped to pioneer such marketing ventures as vegetable box schemes, farmers markets, farm shops and dedicated supply chains from farm to mill, we have today an organic marketplace that is almost wholly dominated by super and hypermarket chains. Their 'green' credentials include the import of some eighty per cent of organic foods, shipped and flown in from all over the world and from farms that are often as big and as indistinctive as their conventional monocultural lookalikes. Here you will find foods branded as 'organic' which bear no resemblance to the 'unrefined, fresh, local and seasonal' foods that contribute to positive health in nature and humanity.

Of course this is all very nice for the Tescos and Sainsburys of this world. It provides a nice bit of green icing for their dark grey cake. But what does it mean for human health? For the future of the 96 per cent of our farmland that remains dependent on regular doses of toxic agro-chemicals? To the once happy dream of a living, quality food based rural economy and to more birds, bees and insects establishing their habitats amongst our unsprayed species rich fields? To farmers who care?

Organic food and farming was predicated on the belief that something called 'holistic thinking' would grow up along with the species rich meadows and living foods. It was based on the idea that we humans are capable of comprehending, even participating in, the cyclic wheel of nature, seasons and unforced productivity. But only a little way down the line, it seems that we lost the plot. Conventional thinking and the greed which comes with power got its way once again.

We are now fast approaching a state in which a two-tier food culture will become the norm. The financially secure and generally privileged will choose a premium priced, largely pesticide free 'organically raised' diet, while those less fortunate will have to contend with factory farmed, hydroponic and genetically modified foods, churned out by corporate enterprises having no other goals other than big profit and domination of the human food chain.

The organic food and farming movement can only challenge this travesty of its original goals if it consciously revisits its roots, both in theory and practice, and ceases to chase the chimera of big-time branded salvation.

4

The Proximity Principle

As a widespread interest in organic food gathered pace in the 1990s, organic farmers and growers found themselves increasingly courted by business conglomerates and institutions that saw the sector as one of the few new areas of commercial opportunity within food and farming.

The way in which organic farmers responded to this courtship has been significant in setting the parameters for the way in which the word 'organic' is now understood and interpreted. Is it seen to reflect the underlying values inherent to the organic farming ethos or simply the efficient and profitable production of 'non-harmful' food by systems that minimise environmental damage?

Over the past decade, it has been a salutary experience to witness the growing momentum of corporate buy-outs of good organic family farm businesses in the British Isles. One after another these once independent enterprises, producing fine foods in sensible, moderate amounts, have fallen to globalised predators in search of a nice 'brand name' and a big-time sales agenda.

However, the globalisation of quality foods comes at a price. This includes loss of authenticity, anonymity, a growing contribution to high food-miles and a heavily packaged and increasingly poor quality end product. The mass production supermarket route is ultimately the antithesis of what 'real food' stands for. There is at least the beginning of some recognition that it is no longer possible to sustain a healthy society while simultaneously trying to squeeze out the last ounce of profit through the pollution and exhaustion of natural resources and the slide from quality to quantity. But this sort of awareness has not spread into mainstream agricultural practices. Clearly a radical action plan is needed if ecologically sound independent farms are to survive in such an alien world.

So far, no fully coherent vision of the way through has emerged. However the re-emerging interest in regional and local foods may provide a means of turning a crisis into an opportunity, through the development a rural resource policy that places 'food sovereignty' above food sales. At the heart of this change will need to be political recognition that reliance upon an increasingly cut-throat and unstable world food market will ultimately leave a high percentage of UK farms uncompetitive, and that the re-emergence of strong local and regional food markets offer a viable alternative.

At the national level, someone with a bit of vision has to recognise that a country needs to be able to feed its own people. Reliance upon a stable import/export market looks increasingly unrealistic as the global economy teeters on the brink of a major collapse. There are a number of potential formulas for developing a sound food security and food sovereignty policy, but the following example, which I call 'The Proximity Principle' offers a practical way forward.

Take a typical market town, population say 12,000. Establish what area of land immediately surrounding the population centre could provide its residents with all their primary food requirements, i.e. vegetables, fruit, meat, dairy and cereal products. A generous but reasonable estimate might reveal that this is approximately an acre per person (12,000 acres). To minimise the impact of transport and pollution and to ensure optimum freshness and nutritional quality, growing and supplying food from the nearest 12,000 acres of productive land should be the primary aim. This offers great opportunities for farmers and growers to form closer links with the citizens they are supplying and to have a secure market right on their doorstep.

After that, each district or county can repeat the formula. Those that have a short-fall, can acquire their quota from the nearest areas having a surplus – and so on. Imagine this process spreading out across the land so that eventually thousands of towns, villages and communities are all drawing from their own hinterlands for their basic needs, and then sharing from each other when there is a surplus or deficit. Something resembling 'life' might once again return to the countryside of the British Isles. This is also the way to ensure the absolute minimisation of waste and a revival of fresh and 'on your doorstep' healthy food.

Only when the whole country is shown to be unable to provide sufficient resources to cater for the needs of its citizens, would imports be triggered, and these should be from the nearest country with a surplus – not from the other end of the world.

The attractions of the town or village market place, architecturally designed for immediate access to the surrounding countryside, are commonly ignored by most town councils when considering planning developments. However they are the obvious place to meet any requirement for a fresh food 'market'. Of course not all produce needs to be sold at an open market, it can go through small shops, direct deliveries and other outlets, but we should not ignore the aesthetic and sensuous appeal of texture, colour, aroma and trading buzz that draws us to the food markets of continental Europe and to the new farmers' markets that have now gained a solid UK foothold.

But the principle should not stop at food. We know we need to move away from our current dependency on finite fossil fuels. In much of the countryside, the potential for local renewable resource exploitation is almost wholly ignored. Local authorities might be amazed to find that their market towns also have the capacity to draw virtually all their energy requirements from sustainable local resources. These will be comprised of a biomass, methane, solar and wind power combination, supplemented (initially) by fossil fuel input. Short coppice willow, woodland off-cuts, waste heat/power exchange and bio-gas extraction should also be developed since the basis for their use is already at hand, but largely unexploited.

This is perhaps the only sane way of overcoming the otherwise intractable problems associated with large scale wind farms and vast arrays of solar panels taking over the sanctity and special characteristics of local countryside features. Forget forever that monstrous ticking time bomb called nuclear power; it is a complete anathema to anybody with an ounce of compassion for the planet. Only human scale developments hold the key to providing human scale solutions. The 'inhuman' ones are not solutions at all.

Assessing and establishing a town's requirement for local foods and renewable energy should also involve local expertise. It can even be done in schools where the flowing imagination of the young can be applied to developing a blueprint of a 'self sufficient' town. Job creation is also an important part of the proximity principle; jobs that fulfil human creative potential.

There is nothing to stop fabric and fibre also being extensively produced at the community level. The market town of Burford in Oxfordshire was completely self-sufficient in food, fibre, fuel and fabric up until around 1930. We do not have to do anything particularly extraordinary to expand upon such achievement and still retain a high quality of life.

The context for recommending such sweeping changes is also informed by broader trading distortions which seriously need redressing: the UK currently imports approximately 90 per cent of its timber requirements with its own woodland cover equalling just 7.6 per cent of total land area. This is a gross imbalance and needs long term planning and action to correct. The UK is now importing almost 40 per cent of its food from across the world and is covering once fertile land areas with concrete, much of it for 'second homes' and hypermarkets. The thought that this might be a highly irresponsible capitulation into short term expediency does not seem to have occurred to those who occupy the leather benches at Westminster.

Long distance organic food imports supply some 70 per cent of the UK consumer market. The food miles involved are considerably higher than the 3,000 kilometre supermarket 'shopping trolley' average of conventional foods pointed up by the campaigning organisation Sustain in their now well thumbed 'Food Miles' report.

The UK also still relies far too heavily on mined, finite resources for industrial, agricultural and domestic energy needs. Much is shipped and piped in at very high cost from sources many hundreds if not thousands of miles away. As a result of our profligate consumer society we produce 20 million tons of rubbish (30 per cent paper based) which is dumped into our landfill sites every year. Not only this, we throw out some 40 per cent of all our purchased food. That is surely the ultimate mark of a terminally sick society.

We know it cannot go on. But nevertheless, dealing with the underlying causes of such a destructive system is studiously avoided. Instead, the preference is to deliberate endlessly on whether a plastic or non plastic shopping bag policy should be adopted by 'x' supermarket chain! This debate soon becoming the sole yard-stick for praising or condemning the performance of these bloated materialist totems that dominate the once diverse and community oriented trading patterns of the United Kingdom.

Fortunately, up and down the country little bursts of 'green' activity are heralding a move towards saner and more self-reliant local economies. This process needs to accelerate. The current 'free trade' world market model is using up what remains of global resources at a rate which cannot be sustained and cannot be condoned. It has been stated that we would need five more planet Earths for the entire human population of our present world to share the same 'standards of living' as post-industrial Northern nations. However we don't have five more planet Earths and even if we did, they would soon be destroyed by the mass exploitation and pollution that underpins this infamous 'standard of living' to which the West has become so indulgently accustomed. We are – and have been – living beyond our means for too long.

The Proximity Principle is for a world where people care. In the British context, it is applicable to nearly all county towns and villages; a modified system, in partnership with intense local 'greening' activities, would have to be worked out for large cities, but still based on the principle of matching local supply and demand as much as possible. Only overall surpluses would be available for export and exotics would still be traded on the international market.

We cannot assume that any existing farming or distribution practice fits neatly into this view of 'sustainability'. At many major retailers one can purchase 'ecological/organic' products that may have started their life in well managed fertile soils, but ended up a week later as vitamin depleted, plastic wrapped dead matter. Organic milk for example, can be purchased as pasteurised, homogenised and semi-skimmed, making it a thoroughly de-natured and almost completely indigestible non-food. Yet such milk is certified as 'organic', generally thought to be a symbol of 'quality' and what the International Federation of Organic Agriculture calls "whole-food" nutrition.

This example reveals a thorny ambivalence: On the one hand, the farming method which generates these products is able to demonstrate a genuine concern for the environment, animal welfare and food purity. But on the other – at the point of sale – what the consumer buys is an unhealthy distortion of a natural food. So which is healthier and more sustainable – the 'organic' processed milk in the supermarket or the locally produced and consumed non-organic fresh whole-milk pinta?

Somewhere along the line, the integrity equating organic farming with wholesome and nutritious foods has been broken. We are now approaching a phase in which the integrity of the organic philosophy demands a greater focus on healing such rifts. Failure to seize a bolder vision will mean 'organic' ending up as little more than a "healthy" appendage to the global food market that ultimately fails both the farmer and the consumer. In its origins, ecologically sound nutritious food was synonymous with local, seasonal and fresh. Such 'real food' fits neatly into the criteria and practice of 'the proximity principle'.

It has been possible to put many of the above theories to practice on my estate at Hardwick over a number of years. We have adopted a policy of local sales for the great majority of food produced on the farm and we also sell all estate firewood within a range of just 8 miles from base. Working on the same principle, we have adopted a local wood heating plan for appropriate estate houses – led by the Hardwick House – and have devised a local strategy for the use of estate timber for building projects on the farm and in houses attached to the Estate. We have introduced allotments where local families are able to grow their own food. But there is plenty more to do in order to optimise the use of our extensive local resources. The success of ongoing initiatives will be informed by just how open residents are to further attempts to close the circle and become largely self-reliant upon the surrounding resource base.

The same can be said for my initiation of the Faringdon 'market town experiment' in the year 2000. The objective at inception was to make the market town of Faringdon, in South Oxfordshire, substantially self-sufficient in food, fuel and fibre by 2015. This is a far from impossible goal for a town with a population of 10,000 surrounded by fertile farmland and some 20 local farmsteads. However, although good initial progress was made, it has been stymied by the seemingly inflexible approach of Faringdon Town Council. There is still a belief that the convenience of a local Tesco supermarket is more desirable than a trading regime comprised of local farmers, small shops, markets and direct deliveries to health and taste conscious consumers who care about the way their food and farming neighbours operate their enterprises.

When we consider the present globalisation model's dastardly wastefulness, it seems only logical to make the maximum use of the forgotten potential that exists right in our own back yard. However, I do not advocate entirely shutting out trading with other communities or other nations. I believe some form of trading keeps open the arteries of communication that are necessary – and indeed pleasurable – in terms of global exchange and the fostering of positive international relations.

Striking the right balance is the issue as always. But while we still have some choice in the matter, it is surely best to pull hard towards correction of the massive global trading imbalances that exist today and which cut swathes of destruction everywhere they turn their profit obsessed attention. Where it occurs, the reawakening of skills associated with local craftsmanship and entrepreneurial creativity at the community level shines as a beacon of hope in the midst of a sea of stultifying and largely destructive mediocrity.

5

Letters to Consumers and Farmers

Consumers:

Listen – do you want to have a full and healthy life? Do you want to have something edible on your plate?

Do you seriously believe that what you currently buy from Tesco and other hypermarkets is actually providing you with your nutritional needs? Do you even care? Or are you 'too busy to think about it'? Do you ever read the labels on the packaging or is it only the price tag that interests you?

Do you know what all those 'E' numbers are or mean? The synthetic preservatives, colours, sweeteners and additives which form a significant part of the 'food' you eat – do you realise what they are doing to you and your children and your grandchildren?

Well I'll tell you: they are destroying your immune systems. They are eating away at your natural resistance to disease. They are hardening your arteries. They are blocking up the valves of your heart. They are contributing to the chances of getting cancer. Have you noticed that people are getting sick more and more frequently? If you haven't noticed you must have been asleep for the past decade. How many times have you felt "really well" recently? Not often? Have you wondered why?

Do you take an interest in the quality of what you put in your belly? Yes? Then why do you still go to those huge supermarket stores that sell you junk food wrapped up in pretty packaging? Did you know that the 'fresh food' they sell you is seldom less than 5 days old? That it has often travelled half way around the world before it gets to you? That it is coming from huge monocultural fields whose soils have been soused with pesticides, herbicides, fungicides and nitrates? You don't know what

29

nitrates are? They are toxic, synthetic stimulants that force plants to grow faster and bigger than they would naturally. All large scale commercial farmers use them. The residues from these nitrates land up in our drinking water – and therefore in our bellies – and so do the pesticide residues, herbicide residues and fungicide residues. So do you begin to get the picture?

But that's not all. Whenever you buy those bakery products chances are you are getting genetically modified (GM) soya added to the flour – and ever wondered what that might be doing to you, slowly, over many years? No? Well, nor it seems, do the transnational corporations that profit from the sales. But we have strong evidence that they are contributing to the loss of your natural reproductive powers – yes – bringing about sterility. Are you willing to risk this most precious gift of reproduction by ingesting GM residues?

But wait! I have even more alarming news for you: the ingestion of GM residues has recently been found to alter the DNA of our gut – the intestinal tracts. GM ingredients are not only in bakery products, but in commercial beers, cooking oils and many other products. They also come through in the milk, meat and eggs from farm animals that are being fed a diet of GM soya and maize – and that is the great majority of herds and flocks in commercial agriculture today.

Did you know that the British government has put off banning the import of genetically modified animal feeds? That they haven't even officially banned the growing of GM crops? In fact they are strongly promoting their development. Are you going to turn the other way and allow your government quietly to permit the irreversible genetic pollution of your food chain and beautiful countryside? Or will you get involved in preventing such a tragedy from ever happening?

Then what about all the refined white flour and sugar in these bakery foods? And what about this so called 'flour' – do you know how much wheat there is in most loaves of bread? Neither the government nor the manufacturers are going to tell you in a hurry, because if they did you would probably stop buying it. What about what is called 'confectionary', do you let your children loose on the rows of junk food confectionary that line the supermarket shelves? Do you want to turn them into mindless and obese beings unable to control their emotions or concentrate for more than a minute at a time? Well?

Now then, I see some of you are still not convinced. If you don't care what you put in your own and your children's stomachs, then perhaps you do at least care about what and who you are supporting when you purchase your food? You might care to know that when you buy this 'stuff' that passes for food in the big supermarkets and in many other shops unfortunately – you are directly supporting what is known as 'factory farming'.

Factory farming: those two words should make you feel a little sick. So I explain. It is the mass production of foods using techniques that are just about as inhumane as one could get. In the case of commercial meat, the pigs and chickens that provide a high percentage of all meat eaten in Europe and North America are raised in animal concentration camps. Their food is typically composed of genetically modified (maize and soya) that has been grown on vast sterile fields somewhere in the USA, Canada, Argentina, China or Brazil, crops that also demand large additions of agrichemicals to ensure their growth.

Then they are crushed for animal consumption and have antibiotics and other synthetic ingredients and fillers added to them. The hens and the pigs that are fed this toxic mix are kept in vast sheds with little or no access to daylight or the outdoors. They have no proper space to move. They cannot roam or play, and live out their brief lives on concrete floors under harsh neon lights. How long do they live? The fattening pigs live for four months and the hens approximately three months. Egg laying hens might live for one year at most.

Then they get slaughtered – in their millions. Humanely

31

raised chickens can easily live happy lives for five years or more and pigs considerably longer. But, dear supermarket consumer, you would really rather not know all this. You would rather prefer to believe the lovely adverts on TV which show contented hens running around in some field and smiling piggies gobbling buckets of delicious mash in their straw covered yard. That's how they sell us the message about our food. And you swallow their sugary virtual reality message without ever questioning it?

Every time you do this you are not only ruining your natural health, you are consciously choosing to give your support to an inhumane factory farm – and to the corporations that manufacture the GM foods and agrichemicals – and to the vast supermarket chains that purchase this sad, sterile food, in full knowledge of the way it is raised.

You see, we are complicit in the establishment of these vast profit making prisons. They wouldn't exist if we didn't support them through buying their produce. WE are the ones who condemn these animals to a life of purgatory. WE are the ones who, by choosing 'not to know' give *carte blanche* to huge corporations to take over control of the food chain and of our own lives. WE are submitting ourselves to becoming slaves to systems that are beneath the basic dignity of both the human and animal kingdom.

Yet many of you recognise the role animals play within the greater family of humankind and live in hope that we might live together as an extended family. But is the factory farm sort of domination of the animal kingdom something you would be happy to support if you actually stopped to think about it? Well?

For God's sake wake up! There are choices that need to be made here. Not making them is not an option any more. It's time to act. Human health, planetary health and universal health are not separate: they are inseparably connected. Take action! Go to your local farmer and ask him or her to grow your own food for you the natural way – without the poisons used on the big commercial farms. Or grow it yourself. Go on – what is the harm in trying?

Farmers:

Is it true that you don't care about the quality of what you cultivate and raise from the land? Or is it that you are happy for your government and agrichemical sales agents to tell you what to grow and how to grow it? Or is it the corporation you buy your seeds from? Or is it the financial subsidies on offer from the European Union that control your thinking? Or are you afraid of being different from your neighbour? Is it perhaps just easier to plod on in the same old way in the hope that somehow you will get by?

Just beyond your door step are many people who could greatly benefit from getting the majority of their daily food needs from you – with no middle man. Of course, they would want this food to be of a good quality: fresh and flavourful and free from harmful residues. This is something the supermarkets can't provide. They are operating through centralised packaging and distribution centres involving hundreds, if not thousands, of kilometres of road haulage. Nothing they provide is fresh, nor is it of any comparable quality to local food. Yet, for some reason you would rather accept the pitiful price the supermarket pays you than get yourselves organised and sell at a fair price to your own community or nearest town?

In the not so distant past, there were proper local processing plants and abattoirs and even help in distribution. But the EU doesn't like small and medium scale self-sufficient units that look after local people with good quality fresh food. Instead it favours large scale monocultural farms employing as few people as possible and turning out thousands of tons of bland, lifeless foods to be sold in some vast bland and lifeless superstore at the other end of the country.

The EU and your government want farmers to be business

people, so that they can be taxed and provide a decent revenue to fill the coffers of central government. What have you been doing for the past ten years? Listening to your 'farmers' union'? Do you think they aren't kowtowing to the EU and the government too?

It is time for us all to come to our senses. The EU, the corporations and the government want you out of the way unless you are already an 'industrial agriculturalist'. They will get you trapped into feeling you 'can't do anything' accept follow their master plan. They will try and make you feel guilty for doing something which is sensible, viable and right. They will throw the 'hygiene and sanitary' rule book at you and tell you to fill in the latest compliance form. They will try and cow you into feeling that you have to conform to their abhorrent global food marketing regime that has the net effect of killing off all the real family farms of Europe and replacing them with 'super-farms' owned and operated by banking cartels.

There's got to be a better way, hasn't there? I mean, if you want any of your children to take an interest in the farm do you really expect them to conform to an EU and government rule book which is written by people who have never set foot on a farm in their lives? Aren't you feeling a bit foolish going along with this sort of rubbish?

If a bunch of locals came to you and asked you to grow some food for them – what would you do? Set the dog on them? Swear at them? Tell them that it's not allowed? Or might you perhaps invite them in for a cup of tea and a chat? Well, if you did, it just could be the starting point for a very interesting possibility. I mean, if these people offered you a fair price to grow some food for them or produce some milk or cheese or whatever it might be – then wouldn't it be a bit foolish to turn them down? They get what they want and you get what you need – a secure local market – and not one controlled by some transnational corporation that wants to screw you. Have a think about it. But don't think too long otherwise you will probably convince yourself that "it's not possible." It's this attitude that keeps us slaves and simply leads to things getting worse and worse.

Consumers and Farmers:

In this letter I have addressed both food buyers and food producers: so now it's down to you. Get together and take control of your destinies; or stay apart and be killed off by transgenic laboratory foods, industrial farming cartels and sold-out corrupted governments. The choice is yours.

6

Who Owns the Food Chain?

We appear to be entering a vortex between two worlds of food and farming. One end of that vortex is firmly planted in the dominant model of the past half-century, with its science guided, laboratory-led, corporately controlled neo-colonial global ambitions. The other end reaches into radically different territory where local and regional food cultivation and distribution fans out across countries increasingly committed to food sovereignty and resource conservation. Which of these models ultimately perseveres is largely down to us – because we are still fortunate enough to eat food virtually every day of our lives and are in a good position to demand that this food is of a quality suitable to genuinely nourish our body and soul. However at almost any time, outside events could intervene in making a significant part of this choice for us. Be they increasingly high fuel prices, catastrophic weather events or even extreme attempts to wrest control over the food chain by dominant corporate cartels hell bent on absolute world dominance.

Unfortunately, it is still a relatively small percentage of individuals who take the trouble to cultivate a discerning view about what they eat and how their food is grown; and it is this more than anything else which allows factory farming and agrichemical conglomerates to retain their stranglehold over around 90 per cent of the western world's food chain. We have been indoctrinated to believe that human, animal and environmental health are somehow 'luxuries' that must take second place to the continued rape of planetary resources for the maintenance of the essentially moribund 'growth at all costs' economic model so blindly adhered to by those who exercise the levers of power.

The UK has been a leading exponent of this materialistic ethos ever since the industrial revolution burst into the rolling fields and meadows of our erstwhile 'green and pleasant land'. The agricultural policy setters who once lived within the hallowed walls of Westminster have long since departed to be replaced by European Union technocrats, large agribusiness concerns and pharmaceutical cartels. There is no 'agricultural policy', merely pressure groups vying for the dominant market position and manipulating government to support their agendas.

Within UK policy-making, government embraces the view that the genetic engineering of crops, seeds and animals takes precedence over support for ecologically benign agricultural systems. This, even after recent independent laboratory research in France revealed shocking evidence of rodents eating GM soya and maize diets developing giant tumours, kidney failure and suffering early deaths.

Here in the UK, we see the need to show a profit by turning once reasonably managed family farms into competing businesses, vying with each other to become mega-sized production units of the sort that dominate the mid-west of North America.

The average size of a UK dairy herd today is approximately 70 cows. Thirty years ago it was 25 and all the cows had names. Now there is a movement towards mega-dairies: in Lincolnshire, for example, there was an application to build units for anything between 3,000 and 8,000 cows. This application was turned down in the short term, but it is evidence of an emerging trend and such developments have already taken place in the United States.

The scale and factory style technology proposed for these mega-dairies would mean that cows would join commercially raised indoor pigs and chickens as nothing more than units on a conveyor belt designed to extract the maximum amount of milk from the cheapest available high protein diet. This diet (as, once again, we have seen from the American example) will be laced with antibiotics and composed of genetically modified soya, maize and quite possibly nanotech feed components as supplementary ingredients. In the UK we think it's clever to copy the United States and apply Ford motor company principles to the management of sentient livestock. However the implications are quite horrific to anyone who has a serious interest in the animals under their care.

Corporate UK is not alone in ignoring the basic rules of good husbandry and human and environmental health. All across Europe, the Common Agricultural Policy of the European Union continues to promote efficient factory farming as the way forward. Exponents, faced by a swelling tide of consumer resistance, turn time and again to the following mantra: "We must be able to feed the world. By 2050 there will be nine billion people on our planet, and only by exploiting the most advanced technologies will we be able to provide them all with adequate amounts of food". There is a shocking degree of duplicity and arrogance in this propaganda which is continuously rolled out by GM corporations, governmental bodies and pseudo scientists in equal degree. It needs to be challenged head-on because it has nothing to do with benevolent concern for the human race and everything to do with maintaining profit-driven industrial agriculture's domination of the food chain.

All the serious evidence points to the opposite conclusion: it is only by nurturing small to medium sized mixed family farms that practise environmentally benign and humane land management systems that communities all over the world will be able to feed themselves and countries develop acceptable levels of food sovereignty/food security. The carefully researched and widely acclaimed International Assessment of Agricultural Knowledge, Science and Technology (IAASTD) report of 2006/7 laid to rest the spurious claims that only genetically modified, nanotech and hydroponically raised crops – produced on vast monocultural prairies and endless rows of soil-less glass laboratories – can be relied upon to provide our daily nourishment. We need to remind ourselves that the 400 international agronomists and scientists who composed the report came down firmly on the side of the small and medium sized mixed family farm coupled to localised distribution patterns as the best bet for feeding the swelling numbers expected on this planet.

But perhaps the most damning of reports was that issued in January 2013 by the Institute of Mechanical Engineers which reveals that almost 50 per cent of the world's food is thrown away and therefore never reaches its destination. That piece of deeply shocking yet vital information has blown a huge hole in the spurious argument that more and more intensive and dubious technologies are needed in order to 'feed the world'.

There are many daunting challenges facing even the most thoughtful farmers and gardeners today, not least the extraordinary plight of our honey bees. As bees throughout Europe and North America continue to succumb to what is termed 'colony collapse disorder' the starkest warning yet of the plight of our food production systems stands apocalyptically before us.

Over the past decades commercial bee colonies have been developed along similar lines to livestock and seeds: they have been hybridized to produce maximum volumes of honey at the lowest possible cost. The great majority have their own version of factory farms to contend with. Their sanitised hives are sprayed with powerful insecticide chemicals, their diet reduced to that which can be foraged from standardised plantations of oilseed crops, themselves subjected to high doses of herbicides, insecticides and fungicides. The hives are transported hither and thither over miles of motorways that link commercial fruit and vegetable farms, each of which demands pollination. All this is further compounded by the addition of copious volumes of refined white sugar to their honey factory hives.

Attempts to nail one predominant cause of the mass die-offs are currently focussing on a particularly insidious insecticide widely sprayed on crops typically foraged by commercial honey bees. Germany has moved to ban this product (supplied by the company BASF) and environmental organisations in other countries are following suit. However, genetically modified organisms (GMOs) are also possible culprits – then what about the atmospheric aerosol spraying that goes on day after day above our heads? What about the vast proliferation of mobile phone masts and associated electromagnetic microwaves? Bees – and many birds – use electromagnetic frequencies to steer their flights between hives and nesting places – could our love affair with the mobile phone be distracting their subtle sense of direction?

Governments are failing to act with any sense of urgency in this increasingly dramatic situation. They remain broadly resistant to the warnings, not daring to offend their paymasters and political allies. And here lies the rub: how can we ever change the rules of the game if those in charge of the rule book have little or no desire to count the true costs of industrial agriculture? Furthermore, time and again we see our political figureheads adopting the solution that offers the best financial return and the least prospect of threat to their cosy power base.

In Poland, where I work with Jadwiga Lopata at the International Coalition to Protect the Polish Countryside, the farming community is just realising what it means to seek to gain advantage from the CAP subsidies on offer to EU member states. Under the current subsidy scheme payments are made on a per hectare basis throughout Europe: so the largest farms are best rewarded and the smallest farms get the crumbs. Such a system could only have been devised by power cartels and technocrats intent on preserving the distorted status quo. How this translates on the ground for Poland, Romania and other Eastern European newcomers is into intense pressure on small farms of around 2 to 15 hectares – of which there are 1.5 million in Poland – to remain solvent in the face of skewed market forces that highlight the financial advantage of being big and brutal.

Foreign corporations have moved into Poland and bought up large tracts of formerly co-operative government land thereby guaranteeing themselves comfortable subsidy-based profits even if next to no food production takes place on their newly acquired assets. The best of such land becomes the venue for intensive agrichemical based arable cropping that quickly drains the soil of its natural fertility and undercuts the market value of produce from smaller farmers still utilising traditional rotations and unable to benefit from the vast economies of scale enjoyed by their competitors. There is the additional grim prospect of EU accepted GM foods being grown on large tracts of land owned by the government and sold on to foreign multinationals.

It is companies like Tesco that become the main beneficiaries of this patently biased EU subsidy regime. They can acquire hundreds of tons of produce from single specialised farm units that will use all the chemical tricks of the trade to ensure that their cereals, potatoes, cabbages, fruits and livestock conform to the exact specification that the supermarkets demand and which can be supplied at prices so low that only very large volumes ensure financial viability. It is these farms/farmers who are most eagerly targeted by corporate agribusiness monsters like Monsanto, Cargill, Dupont, Pioneer, BASF, Bayer, Cyngenta et al. It does not require a particularly hard sell to get many farmers to sign up to lobby for GM crops and seeds. To insist on the spurious notion that GM animal feeds comprising largely genetically modified soya and maize should be the staple diet of their mass production animal factories and the vast intensive indoor pig units that operate under the aegis of transnational giants like Smithfield and Danish Crown.

So bad is the food quality of products emanating from such animal and cereal concentration camps that I would hesitate to call it 'food'. So depleted of vitamins and energy and so lacking in flavour are the majority of products emerging from these enterprises (let's not call them 'farms') that they can only be successfully marketed by utilising the skilful propaganda tactics and virtually bottomless advertising budgets transnational corporate food distributors have at their disposal. Products which are essentially worthless in terms of their nutritional value can be made to look like wonderful fresh foods that every modern housewife must surely want on her family table. Given the right marketing regime and peak time television airspace, almost anything is possible.

Through successfully manipulating these powers, the combined forces of the World Trade Organisation, the World Bank, the European Union, agrichemical conglomerates and 'Big Pharma' (as the pharmaceutical giants are collectively known) have pretty much stitched up the food chain from farm to fork throughout the so-called developed world. Now the only options for those unwilling to sell their souls and degrade their soils are to try to operate beneath the radar or start another ball game on another pitch, and try to attract enough discerning citizens to support their efforts to ensure their survival. There are many signs that seem to show such a resistance movement is getting under way, albeit sporadically, in many parts of the UK and on the continent of Europe.

The peasant support group La Via Campesina which claims a membership of some 40 million peasant farmers mostly in South America, has now set up also in Spain and France. The organisation has its European office in Brussels and promotes food sovereignty and respect for the role of small farmers in maintaining the biodiversity of traditional European foods, ecologies and indigenous non-hybrid seeds.

Carlo Petrini's Slow Food movement has now spread around the world and is encouraging peasants to hold on to their artisan skills in the face of the sterilisation and globalisation of once vibrant, living indigenous foods. In France, Les Faucheurs (the Reapers) have succeeded in blocking any further attempts to cultivate the GM maize MON 810 and have managed to infiltrate a number of commercial and government laboratories working on GM seed research projects. Public pressure in almost all of mainland Europe remains firmly against GM food and farming. Seven Countries have managed to ban MON 810 GM maize. Opinion polls in the UK continue to indicate a majority saying 'No to GMO'.

Yet this has not stopped the European Commission from trying to foist responsibility for decisions of whether or not to accept GM plantings of those varieties already accepted for cultivation in Europe (mainly maize and now a potato for starch) on individual member states. The European Parliament's committee for Agriculture and the Rural Economy is pressing ahead with proposals to ensure that each member state sets its own specific 'co-existence' rules, thus backing the WTO's demand of 'freedom of choice' for farmers to plant GM crops if they wish. 'Co-existence' is a classic Trojan Horse. It allows GM crops to be planted next to conventional and organic crops with only a 30 metre intervening strip of land acting as a barrier – thereby virtually ensuring cross-contamination and the demise of a largely GM free Europe.

Meanwhile, waiting in the wings, are some 500 patent applications for so called 'climate ready' GM seeds and plants. These seeds are designed to operate in conditions of drought and flood and to displace altogether the traditional seeds that are saved and planted by the great majority of small farmers and gardeners the world over. They are all untested scams and have no place whatsoever in any genuine agricultural policy.

Demonstrations against industrial agriculture and GM foods have attracted significant numbers of concerned citizens. On 21 January 2011, 20,000 protesters congregated in Berlin to expose the Angela Merkel government's continued support for GM crops and corporate control of the food chain. Under the banner 'We have had enough!' they demanded a return to small-scale, localised and ecological food and farming practices and genuine food autonomy at the grass roots level. The protest was timed to coincide with a high-level meeting on global agricultural policies attended by Pascal Lamy, the head of the World Trade Organisation.

The International Coalition to Protect the Polish Countryside demonstrated solidarity with this protest by initiating 'Support the Traditional Countryside' actions in 90 venues throughout Poland, attracting much interest and support. ICPPC catalyses regular protests against GM seeds and plants to build greater public awareness and bring pressure for a complete GMO ban into the political agenda of the country.

The Polish government is trying to play to both corporate and social interests at the same time. It continues to sell off state agricultural land to the highest foreign bidders while claiming to be protecting the interests of its own farming communities. On GM issues, it has failed to take any decisive action for fear of upsetting the EU to whom it is increasingly kowtowing.

I cannot do justice to the numerous autonomous ecological initiatives patiently working for positive change. As corporate attempts to take total control of the food chain appear to be tightening their grip, so too does the awareness of this threat appear to be growing. There is no doubt that the battle lines are being drawn. The Codex Alimentarius ('International Food Standards') stick wielded by the World Trade Organisation and seamlessly passed on by the European Commission is attempting to crush the right of family farmers the world over to produce and sell the products of their own farms unless they conform to ever more draconian and increasingly arbitrary sanitary and hygiene measures. Even seed saving and redistribution is now heavily restricted, with large fines threatened for anyone daring to make commercial use of any seeds not on the super hybrid official EU 'seed list'. Compliance with such demands bankrupts most traditional family farming enterprises and ensures the placement of such farms on the market where hungry corporate predators are ready to swoop in and sweep them up, setting in motion the factory farming regimes that are tied in with the leading super-market chains of North America and Europe.

On my own farm in the UK (Hardwick), I have set in motion a scheme to let local people grow their own food on a 2.5 acre site previously rented out as a horse paddock. We have 25 families already well-installed on subdivisions of the field and another 6 acres is being allocated to 2 small holding initiatives. I believe that this marks a turning point and possible watershed for a radically new direction for the procurement of high quality, fresh, seasonal and local food. It marks the start of 'Farming for the People with the People' as the only way forward for all those determined not to become slaves to a robotic, inhuman and exploitative system of global cartels that will stop at nothing to achieve its ambitions of exerting total control of the food chain, thereby imposing a form of dietary genocide on the population of this planet.

Rejection of this nightmare vision is now a matter of urgency.

7

The Battle to Save the Polish Countryside

Poland is accustomed to fighting rear guard actions to free itself from unwelcome invaders. Throughout what are known as "The Partitions", a nineteenth-century period of occupation by Russia, Prussia and Austria, Poles kept in their hearts a longing for a day when they could be freed from the yoke of repression and find genuine independence. After finally succeeding, in 1918, to rid themselves of the unloved invaders, they were soon engulfed in conflict again – this time with invading Nazi Germany – and responded by courageously establishing the renowned 1939-45 'resistance movement' which sprouted-up in the fields, small towns and main cities, producing much heroic action.

As many will know, Poles fought alongside the British throughout the Second World War – a time when Poland's government in exile had its headquarters in London. I remember quite well, when I was a boy, a Polish exile who lived in our village (Whitchurch-on-Thames) coming regularly to my family home and diligently cleaning the chimneys. He spoke little, but did a very thorough job.

It was only in 1989 that Poland finally threw off the last repressive regime of occupation in their land, the Russian communists. So, the last nineteen years of freedom have been the longest historical period of non-occupation for a very long time.

The Nobel prize winning author, Thomas Mann, who fled from Nazi Germany just prior to World War Two, remarked just before he died (in 1969) that he feared that although the Nazis had been defeated, fascism had not: " I am concerned about the weak position of freedom in post-World War Two Europe and North America" he is reported to have observed.

We can surely identify with his concern for 'the weak position of freedom' is insidiously manifesting itself throughout our increasingly pacified society – and it has recently come to undermine the long standing traditions of the Polish countryside, and particularly the independence of the peasant and family farms and the hugely biodiverse Polish countryside of which they are the prime trustees.

The Communists failed to quell the small Polish peasant farmers into submission during their period of occupation, which left the country with a rich, if rather confusing, legacy of approximately one and a half million small scale family farms (average size 18 acres) dotted around the Polish Provinces, but particularly prevalent in the south and east.

When I was first invited (November 2000) by Jadwiga Lopata, founder of The International Coalition to Protect the Polish Countryside (ICPPC), to come to Poland as a co-director of this newly established non-governmental organisation, the country was preparing itself – or more correctly was 'being prepared for' entry into the European Union. Opinions were strongly divided concerning the merits of such an action and those most against included the farmers.

One of our first tasks, as I saw it, was to warn Poles just what 'joining the EU' would mean for the farming population, for rural communities and for the renowned biodiversity of the countryside. Under the auspices of a senior civil servant in Warsaw, Jadwiga and I were able to address a meeting with the Brussels based committee responsible for negotiating Poland's agricultural terms of entry into the EU. It proved to be an ominous foretaste of things to come.

The first thing that struck us was the fact that out of the twelve people sitting in the room at the European Commission, not one was Polish. I explained to the attendant body that in a country where 22 per cent of the working population are involved in agriculture – and the majority on small farms – it would not be a good idea to follow the same regime as had been operated in the UK and other EU member countries, in which 'restructuring' agriculture had involved throwing the best farmers off the land and amalgamating their farms into large scale monocultural operations designed to supply the predatory supermarket chains. You could have heard a pin drop.

After clearing her throat and leaning slowly forward, the Chairwoman said: "I don't think you understand what EU policy is. Our objective is to ensure that farmers receive the same salary parity as white collar workers in the cities. The only way to achieve this is by restructuring and modernising old fashioned Polish farms to enable them to compete with other countries' agricultural economies and the global market. To do this it will be necessary to shift around one million farmers off the land and encourage them to take city and service industry jobs to improve their economic position. The remaining farms will be made competitive with their counterparts in western Europe."

There, in a nutshell, you have the whole tragic story of the clinically instigated demise of European farming over the past three decades. We opined that with unemployment running at 20 per cent how would one provide jobs for another million farmers dumped on the streets of Warsaw? This was greeted with a stony silence, eventually broken by a lady from Portugal, who rather quietly said that since her country had joined the European Union, sixty per cent of small farmers had already left the land. She then added: "The European Union is simply not interested in small farms."

A month or so after this encounter, we were invited to the Polish parliament to address the government's agricultural committee. I gave a speech entitled "Don't Follow Us" in which I explicitly warned what fate was in store for the Polish countryside if Poland joined the EU. I gave some vivid examples of what had happened in the UK over the past two decades: the ripping up of 35,000 miles of hedgerows; the loss of 30 per cent of native farmland bird species; 98 per cent of species-rich hay meadows, thousands of tons of wind and water eroded topsoil and the loss from the land of around fifteen thousand farmers every year, accompanied by a rapid decline in the quality of food.

That night *Rzeczpospolita*, a leading national broadsheet, carried a portion of this speech under the intended heading "Don't Follow Us". The piece appeared in exactly half the editions, in the other half was an article praising the merits of Poland joining the EU. That was in the autumn of 2001.

Poland joined the EU in 2004 after an intense publicity campaign calling upon Poles to "Say Yes to the EU!". The propaganda machine went into overdrive with brash promises of "pots of gold" being showered on Poland and farmers being offered generous agricultural subsidies and free advice, provided they played by the rules of the game.

That 'game' was all too familiar to me:

- Spending hours out of your working day filling in endless forms, filing maps and measuring every last inch of your fields, tracks and farmsteads;
- Applying for 'passports' for your cattle and ear tags for your sheep and pigs;
- Resisting the slurry pit and putting stainless steel and washable tiles on the dairy walls. Becoming versed in HACCP (Hazard Analysis and Critical Control Points) hygiene and sanitary rules and applying them where any food processing was to take place;
- Living under the threat of convictions and fines should one put a finger out of place or be late in supplying some official details.

Throughout this time, I clearly remember the sense of losing something intangible, something more valuable than that which was gained on the eventual arrival of the subsidy cheque. What we were losing was our independence and our freedom; the slow rural 'way of life' shared by traditional farming communities throughout the world. You cannot put a price on this immeasurably important quality. It is a deep, lasting and genuinely civilised expression of life.

So now that the Poles, with their two million family farms, were going to be subjected to the same fate, Jadwiga and I felt desperate to try and avert this tragedy. An uphill struggle ensued, which involved swimming strongly against the tide of the agribusiness and seed corporations who were gleefully moving in behind the mantle of EU free trade agreements and a government that had capitulated to the demands of the corporations and Brussels.

What these corporations want (I use the present tense as the position remains the same today) is to get their hands on Poland's relatively unspoiled work force and land resources. They want to establish themselves on Polish soil, acquire their capital cheaply and flog the end products of Polish labour to the rest of the world for a big profit. Farmers stand in the way of land based acquisitions and so they are best removed. Corporations thus join with the EU in seeing through their common goals and set about intensively lobbying national government to get the right regulatory conditions to move in for the kill.

The farmers, once having fallen for the CAP subsidy carrot, suddenly find themselves heavily controlled by EU and national officialdom brandishing that most vicious of anti-entrepreneurial weapons: 'sanitary and hygiene regulations' – as enforced by national governments on the behest of the Common Agricultural Policy of the European Union. These are the hidden weapons of mass farmer destruction and the main tool for achieving the CAP's aim of ridding the countryside of small and medium sized family farms and replacing them with fully commercialised agribusiness.

Already by 2005, 65 per cent of regional milk and meat

processing factories had been forced to close because they 'failed' (read couldn't afford) to implement the prescribed sanitary standards. Some 70 per cent of small slaughter houses have also suffered the same fate. Farmers increasingly have nowhere to go to sell their cattle, sheep, pigs and milk. Exactly as happened to UK farmers, Polish farmers are now being forced out of business by the covert and overt destruction of the infrastructure which supports their profession. The rural economy thus implodes and farming communities are scattered to the wind. All that emerges on the green fields that they have left behind them are Tesco-style cloned hypermarkets.

The European Union Common Agricultural policy, sanitary and hygiene weapons have already been re-sharpened and, as I write, are busily scything their way through Romanian family farms, whose extraordinary diversity and peasant farming skills match those of their Polish counterparts. Turkish agriculture is in similar danger, too, as a 'modernising' elite seeks economic and cultural convergence with Europe.

What is known as the 'global food economy' is the instrument of a relatively small number of very wealthy transnational corporations. It is a small club, but one which harbours very big ambitions. One such corporation is Monsanto (USA), whose marriage with the Cargill Corporation, makes it the biggest seed and agrichemical merchant in the world. Poland has for some time been in the sights of the Monsanto corporation, as well as fellow seed operatives, Dupont, Pioneer and Syngenta. However, in 2004 – the same year that Poland joined the EU – Monsanto started a major lobbying drive on senior figures in the Polish government. They called for a relaxation of national GMO precautionary laws and a government commitment to supporting the development of genetically modified organisms as a symbol of the modernisation of traditional Polish farming.

We at ICPPC got wind of these developments and decided to put the great majority of our time and the lion's share of our meagre financial resources, into fighting this new and immensely threatening dragon. Thus started an amazing campaign which, over the space of one and a half years, managed to help galvanise the provincial boards of every province in Poland (there are 16) to come up with a "GMO Free Zone" self-declaration. Each province in turn, picked up the torch and signed on, so that eventually (September 2005) the whole country could declare itself 'GMO Free'.

The chairs of each provincial branch of ICPPC wrote to the prime minister demanding national legislation to recognise their new status by law. At first nothing happened, but then, much to everyone's surprise – and Monsanto's fury – Jaroslaw Kaczynski (the then Prime Minister) announced that legislation would be passed to ban the import and sale of GMO seeds and plants in Poland. This was followed a little later by a similar announcement declaring that GM animal feed would also be banned as of 2008.

Europe and the rest of the world were amazed. Seemingly coming out of nowhere there was suddenly a country that had passed national legislation to ban GM seeds and animal feeds, an illegal act in the eyes of the European Commission. Only Greece and Austria had come close to achieving such a barrier. It seemed that Poland was to make history and perhaps lead the rest of Europe towards a new moratorium, if not outright ban, of GMO.

But such a fairy tale scenario has yet to unfold. In fact, the situation has gone into decline. Under the administration of Donald Tusk, the commercial planting of GM seeds is back on the agenda and a new act is proposed to align Poland with Brussels and open the possibility for the 'Coexistence' of GM and non GM crops. Such a plan would spell disaster in the highly diverse Polish countryside and result in the 'cross-contamination' of non-GM crops. ICPPC continues (2010) to battle against this outcome and urge the current administration to follow the example of Germany, France, Austria, Greece, Italy Hungary, Bulgaria and

Luxembourg – and ban GM crops.

Back in 2005, bemused Polish farmers could hardly grasp the significance of attempts to foist genetically modified organisms upon them. Already deeply perplexed by the strange new world of western capitalism and shell shocked by the complexities and apparently two faced nature of the CAP, the additional need to absorb the seemingly unfathomable 'science' and propaganda surrounding GMO, left many confused and uncertain. Aware of this dangerously exploitable situation, we embarked on a country wide awareness raising campaign armed with the anti GMO expose film "Life Running Out of Control" dubbed into Polish and recorded onto Compact Disc.

We ran into considerable levels of opposition, especially wherever university professors of agriculture were invited to lead public debates. Often, on such occasions, Jadwiga and I were the only voices against GMO and were up against half a dozen power point presentation-backed professionals, lecturing (as it often seemed to us) straight from the Monsanto manual! However, the distinctly intuitive Polish public, nearly always came down on our side, offering much needed encouragement.

Newspapers, television and to a lesser extent radio, were – and remain – pretty much gagged from reporting the truth. As we discovered, much of the Polish media is in foreign hands or a high stake is held by outside interests. The GMO lobby had already won round the main Polish farmers union and the new government, under Prime Minister Donald Tusk, kept an increasingly silent position on the future of the anti-GMO legislation enacted by his predecessor.

Kaczynski's team had already appeared to stall when confronted by the dual threat of a fine from the European Commission for instituting an 'illegal' blanket ban on GMO (under EU law no country is allowed to overstep 'free trade' diktats by outright banning GMO) and the huge corporate backlash resulting from the ban. Now that a new government with a distinctly modernising agenda was in charge, we were forced to work even harder in order to keep the anti GMO momentum alive. We therefore decided to help create a new national organisation, The Coalition for a GMO Free Poland, and to draw upon as wide a cross section of society as possible to promote its aims. There are now 180 organisations and key individuals on the books and we have made some headway with the wary media.

Amongst those who have joined up are colleagues fighting another predatory US invader, Smithfield, the giant pig factory farming multinational (UK subsidiary Danish Crown, East Anglia) which moved onto Polish soil (or should I say concrete) in the late 1990s and, with a strong link to Monsanto's North American GM soya export trade, established their perverse animal factories with the aid of a cheap Polish work force and compliant government officials. The thousands of GM soya fattened pigs that now flood the market have helped to undercut the prices and destroy the livelihood of many hundreds of already hard pressed traditional pig farmers throughout Poland and far beyond.

Smithfield and other industrial farming units operating out of Poland do not like the idea of a GM animal feed ban and have used the current high price of conventional animal feeds to pressurise government into postponing the ban to 2009 or beyond. A great opportunity will be lost if this postponement is agreed – and it will be harder to ensure that companies such as Smithfield can be prevented from further exploiting the market-place's demand for cheap pork.

How ironic it is, that the hell bent US development of biofuels has played into the hands of the exponents of cheap, mass produced GMO aided animal flesh production. It has forced up the price of conventional feeds, such as barley based products, through replacing cereal production with millions of acres of GM maize for burning up as fuel for motor cars and trucks. Now GM soya and maize, previously avoided by most European animal feed importers, suddenly look like the only cheap option available. We have consistently lobbied for government to encourage farmers to grow their own traditional feed products, but in a world hooked on the global shipment of cheap proteins, such advice has fallen on deaf ears.

Poland has all the potential for a full blown peasants' revolt to recapture the right to grow, eat and trade their superb farmhouse foods; thus freeing themselves from the increasing stranglehold that the bureaucratic and perverse sanitary and hygiene regulations have imposed. With one and a half million, largely subsistence based, small family farms still in operation, it is something we should not rule out. But perhaps the strongest force militating against such an action is the fact that a fair proportion of farmers have already signed up to the 'pot of gold' held tantalisingly in front of their noses by the Brussels bureaucrats. In reality, this ultimately delivers just a few crumbs of financial support to farms of just five to seven hectares, but rewards large farms with substantial offerings.

Money can indeed buy-out the seeds of revolution but the heart of the peasants will not be satisfied. Neither will the hearts of caring individuals who know and love the working countryside. In a world where genuine independence is seen as a threat to the controlling influence of transnational and national power brokers, a watchful eye will be kept on any potentially rebellious leaders and covert efforts made to ensure that passivity remains supreme. However, we are in for some big changes, some from a poisoned and polluted nature in rebellion, but others by the hands of those who are waking up to the stark choices which confront all of us: capitulate to the forces of authoritarian corporatism masquerading as 'economic liberalism' or wrest back control of life and work to rejuvenate local communities to do the same.

Poland is well versed in the art of survival. Provided that the next generation of farm owners has the will to carry forward the traditions inherited along with the land, there is great hope for this proud and brave nation to come through the chaos with its soul un-bought and its seeds un-modified.

8

Poland, Solidarity and the Third Way: A Time of Destiny

When I read the headline in the UK journal 'Farming News' in the spring of 1989 – I felt a stab of pain in my heart. "Poland Up for Grabs" ran the headline story printed in bold across the front page of this widely distributed British farming journal. Although at the time I had never been to Poland or thought a great deal about this country, the effect that this headline had was quite startling.

I clearly saw thousands of traditional farms, active communities and countryside ways of life, being steamrollered by greedy Western corporate agribusiness with its insatiable appetite for easy profit, new markets and neo-colonial outreach. It seemed impossible that Poland would allow such a fate to overtake it, especially after expending so much heroic energy in ridding itself of decades of Communist oppression. But the headline was real enough and it surely would have sent a shiver down the spine of any Polish patriot.

That same spring, events in the UK had already impacted heavily on my farming operations. In February 1989 the British government suddenly declared that it was going to ban the sale of unpasteurised milk – my main farm business and a life-line enterprise for many small traditional dairy farms. My only recourse was to start a national campaign to try to reverse this decision.

It turned out to be a fast and furious affair lasting just four months and ending in a victory for the producers and consumers of 'real milk'. The government backed down, helped by strong media interest and the fact that Prime Minister Thatcher expressed "some sympathy" for my campaign against the ban.

However, the government still contrived to put a 'health warning' on the product despite the fact that for decades no one had become seriously ill from consuming this living and highly nutritious food.

Poland, however, was facing a crisis on a whole other dimension. Almost ten years after the formation of the Solidarity trade union, the enormous popularity of Lech Walesa and his fellow Gdansk shipyard mates had finally driven the Communists out of the country. The relatively moderate Gorbachev had realised that any further attempts at military suppression were only likely to add further fuel to the fire of rebellion sweeping the country. Suddenly 'Solidarnosc' had achieved its goal and, against great odds, not only dispelled its main oppressor, but won itself a victory in the first free elections as well.

As I was struggling to get my farming operations back on course after a hectic campaign to keep open the market for natural milk, Poles were celebrating world-wide acclaim for their victory over the Communist Party/state machine.

At this pivotal moment in history, events threw open an unprecedented opportunity for a brand new socio-economic vision to take shape amongst the down trodden factories and industries that formed the foundation of the almost 100 per cent state owned Polish economy. The vision was of a workers' cooperative that would take over and run the entire edifice of state manufacturing industry and thereby influence all aspects of the economic welfare of the country.

The implications of this bottom-up grass roots take-over of the economic motor of the country were clearly enormous, not only for Poland but for the rest of the world as well. The new model was called "The Third Way" and would depose the commanding position held by both communism and capitalism should it come to fruition.

The Third Way

I only heard about the Third Way when reading Naomi Klein's book *The Shock Doctrine* (2007). Immediately, I understood that the great responsibility that had been placed on the shoulders of the Solidarity team negotiating Poland's future. The Third Way laid out a mould breaking formula for the future which seemed likely to scare the pants off entrenched doctrines of both West and East. This was not only because it did away with the old communist and capitalist models, but also because it was led by a workers' union with the full support of the people.

The first major hurdle faced by supporters of this vision was how to deal with the huge national debt left by the departing Communist regime. According to Naomi Klein, it stood at $40 billion and an inflation rate running at 600 per cent. Unfortunately for Poland (and the rest of us) the realisation of The Third Way was to be undermined by an argument over how to pay off this debt – and by the intervention in the Solidarity committee of Jeffrey Sachs, the young American academic who was then a protégé of the Chicago School of free-market economists led by Milton Friedman. Friedman's already well tested formula for dealing with this sort of crisis was 'pure' capitalism coupled to the privatisation and sale of state controlled assets. Sachs, whose name had already been made through expounding this doctrine to a heavily economically indebted Bolivia, stood at the opposite end of the political and economic spectrum from Solidarity at that time; yet he was still able to swing the argument in favour of the essentially neo-liberal economic doctrine which continues to hold sway over much of the Western world.

The possibility of a Third Way had first been aired back in 1981. In a paper laying out the plan, Solidarity pioneers stated: "We demand a self-governing and democratic reform at every management level and a new socio-economic system combining the plan (*sic*), self-government and the market ... The socialised enterprise should be the basic organizational unit of the economy. It should be controlled by the workers council representing the collective and should be operatively run (*sic*) by the director, appointed through competition and recalled by the council."

The message was revolutionary enough to unnerve and infuriate Moscow, leading General Jaruzelski, chief of the Polish Army, to send the tanks into the Gdansk shipyard and declare a state of martial law in the country. That state was maintained until the final uprisings of 1989 and the victory of the Solidarity trade union's long running opposition to Soviet occupation.

By then Jeffrey Sachs had succeeded in convincing enough of Solidarity's leading members that only a massive loan from the International Monetary Fund (IMF) would get Poland out of trouble and that by using his contacts he would personally be able to open the IMF door to unlock the needed funds. Many, it seems, were deeply perturbed by this proposal, but others saw no other way of paying off state debts. The resolution to this debacle was as profoundly significant as was the end of Communism: Poles had freed themselves from one great oppressor only to find the door being opened to another.

Sachs was true to his word and the IMF money was put on the table, but only at the price of a mass sell-off of state industries and the adoption of the sort of economic free market policies that remain the hallmark of US global hegemonic ambition – especially when coupled to IMF strategic asset stripping expertise. As the Red Army disappeared from view in the East, so the red white and blue neo-liberal army made its triumphal entry from the West. Tragically, the new economic and political hegemony excluded and obscured any conception of a Third Way.

"Poland Up for Grabs" still haunts me. The spring 1989 Farming News edition sporting this title remains embedded in my mind and I cannot help but reflect on its dark significance.

Among others, UK corporate agriculture was quick to see the opening created by Sachs and his Chicago School of Economics. Former state farms needed new investors and who better than the leading UK practitioners of agrichemical monocultures to take up the offer; soon to be followed by their continental rivals.

Polish soils were still relatively unblemished and fertility levels still well above Western European levels. Here was a great chance to go all out to exploit this fertility and profit from the cheap labour still abundant in newly liberated Poland. British and continental soils were run down after years of high input/high output farming had drained natural nutrient and humus levels making most farmers dependent upon large volumes of toxic synthetic fertilizers and pesticides. Sachs had now paved the way for a foreign mining of Polish soils, the profits of which would flow westwards, along with the relentless interest paid on the IMF loan.

The terrible truth about the widely acclaimed Solidarity victory was that it was simultaneously an almost unbearable defeat for the forces of freedom. The new independence brought with it a new enslavement: the toxic economical and agricultural intervention of the West replaced the brutal politico-military intervention of the East. "Freedom" had proved to be an illusion.

In the early 1990s a shell shocked nation could not easily recognise the true nature of its new masters. Shops filled with Western consumables; Coca Cola became ubiquitous as did McDonalds; the first supermarkets started sprouting up in the big cities and Poles queued outside the American Embassy to get visas to 'the land of liberty'. To the Poles who believed that 'the grass is greener on the other side', the new state of liberation may have looked like some kind of salvation, but to many others the reality belittled the promise that it might initially have held.

In the cities, unemployment started growing fast with wages failing to meet rising costs. In the countryside, the rural economy, well cared for under Communism, imploded, as new regulations based on World Trade Organisation and Brussels EU directives forced the closure of thousands of small and medium sized food processing units, abattoirs and cottage industries. Enterprises that had mostly thrived during the occupation but now were deemed unsuitable for a country in line to become amongst the first of the Eastern European states to join the European Union. Once thriving villages with full employment became victims of global economic capitalism's aggressive competition formulas: a few large centralised corporate manufacturing and processing units displacing thousands of small local enterprises run as cooperatives by resident families.

9

The Pot of Gold and the European Union

As citizens struggled to adjust to this new way of life, Poland's governing bodies became resigned to the next big Western promise. This was the so-called 'pot of gold' to be showered on the country upon achieving the socio-economic standards necessary to assure entry into the European Union. Once again 'the money promise' was moving centre stage and the Polish nation was about to receive its next dose of Western medicine.

I first set foot on Polish soil at around this time. It was in the autumn of 2000 when Jadwiga Lopata invited me to become a co-founder of the International Coalition to Protect the Polish Countryside. In a packed farmhouse in the foothills of the Beskidy Mountains of Southern Malopolska, the ICPPC was born and I was thrust into the centre of a crucial arena of decision making concerning the future. My first thought was to try and ensure that Poland's accession to the EU was properly negotiated, and that the mass exodus from the land that accompanied my own country's (and many others') entry would not be repeated in Poland. A few months later, a senior civil servant in Warsaw made it possible for Jadwiga Lopata and myself to be invited to the European Commission to meet the negotiating team responsible for Poland's agricultural and environmental entry into the EU.

What came out of this meeting was as shocking as anything that had preceded it. The Chairwoman of the committee informed us that Poland was to be stripped of at least one million small and medium sized farms in order to make way for the 'restructuring and modernisation' of its tried and tested traditional agricultural practices. This, it turned out, meant the end of mixed family farms and their replacement by large scale agribusiness conglomerates that would make Polish agriculture 'competitive on the World market'. The committee clearly saw industrial farming as the perfect remedy for Poland's "peasant farming anachronism" and the Chair then declared that it was only a matter of time before such a transformation would be complete. This time, the dogma of Friedman's Chicago School would be applied to the rich bio-diverse meadows of the Polish countryside. (For more details of this meeting, and the founding of ICPPC, see Chapter 8 above.)

With this message still burning in our minds, it seemed essential to put out an immediate alert and warn Polish parliamentarians of what was coming. At a press conference in the Polish parliament some days later, I was able to warn the people of Poland not to fall for the illusory 'pot of gold' which will only further enslave your nation to the ambitions of an unelected supranational foreign body based in Brussels. This cartel had already caused great damage to my own country. Its high tech/low labour policies had already torn apart thousands of virtually self-sufficient communities across the continent of Europe.

Six months after warning the Polish parliament what was in store, the government fell, to be replaced by a pro-EU pro free market political party fully committed to Poland's entry into the European Union by 2004. It was the signal for Poles to be fed an increasingly intense diet of pro-EU propaganda through the mainstream media, with much being made of 'the pot of gold' which Brussels was to bestow upon the outstretched hands of this supposedly impoverished nation. The rest, as they say, "is history." However, it is a history thick with intrigue, deceit and brazen disinformation. Poland's entry into the EU has not lifted the country out of financial indebtedness, nor has it improved the financial position of millions of ordinary workers who have seen the rich get richer and their own wages fail to keep step with rising prices.

At the heart of Poland's dilemma lies a pivotal issue upon which a positive resolution of the nation's destiny still hangs: who can do what the dock workers could not do? Who can introduce a worker owned socio-economic revival based on the Third Way? Who can defeat the corporate and allied political forces whose devious alliance harbours barely hidden ambitions to take absolute control of not only the Polish food chain but the country's entire economic destiny?

Back in 1989, the passionate discourses of Solidarnosc workers had produced what were both an extraordinarily courageous and radical manifesto *and* a pragmatic solution to the immediate issues facing the country. That is surely exactly what is again needed now in 2012, not just for Poland but for the world at large. In fact, everywhere where the outdated and outmoded models of capitalism and communism (and I would add socialism) retain their grip on socio-economic and political agendas.

The Third Way is far too important to be allowed to be swallowed up in historical narrative. It is a dynamic agenda which represents the best chance we have to overcome the phoney politics of our time. Politics which seek to retain their power by dividing and conquering; by setting one faction against another faction; one false ideology against another false ideology; one class against another class: the 'no change' which cunningly masquerades as 'choice'.

The Third Way rises above all this and takes up the vacant centre ground, having the potential to unite national sentiments in the process. It defines what a 'people-led' movement should be and finally gives the politically and economically marginalised centre stage. Powerful banking and corporate industrial cabals that now rule the world will be brought down to earth with a mighty bump once such a movement finds its feet and receives the blessing of the electorate. I believe that time is now at hand and the moment has come for the Solidarity plan, hatched more than 30 years ago, to be brought to fruition.

A Metamorphosis and a Destiny

The year 2012, and the years immediately following, show many auspicious signs suggesting that the suppression of humanity by small groups of power obsessed financiers can be defeated and that fresh 'people-led' actions can rise up to take their place. Poland is well placed to play a leading role in this metamorphosis. There is the potential to unlock the creative powers so long held in check, both by foreign invaders and by (if I may say this as a close friend, but a foreign observer nonetheless) a certain lack of self-belief. These forces have, until now, held back the promise of something far better for this long suffering nation: the realisation of a genuine state of self-determination and cultural flowering so longed for by millions of people from all walks of life.

Such a change is surely well overdue. The valiant struggles and set-backs of the shipyard workers of Gdansk are still to be vindicated, not in the now dismantled yards and factories of the Baltic coast, but amongst the millions of small and medium sized farms that are the last remaining major asset still in the hands of working people. This is an asset which was never captured by the Russian invaders and still remains out of reach of the IMF, the World Bank, the European Commission and the giant agribusiness, pharmaceutical and seed corporations. It is therefore still possible for Poland to avoid the corporate stranglehold that afflicts the Western food chain and the once fertile farmlands of Europe and North America.

It is precisely here where the chance still exists to turn around the fortunes of the Polish nation, and where one finds the last bastion of 'independent' working people stubbornly refusing to give up their land based way of life. These people, who are the true guardians of the 'non-patented' food chain, need our support. Our future health and welfare is literally in their hands. Brussels has so far failed in its attempts to eject one million of such people from the land as the Commission promised back in 2000. The EU master plan is not working in Poland.

Since joining the EU in 2004, around 200,000 farms have gone out of business in Poland.

There still remain close to 1.5 million working farms and the great majority are owned by those who work their soils. Here lies the most fertile ground for the realisation of a plan based around Solidarity's still unrealised Third Way. The implementation of such a plan could prevent these farms being picked off one by one by the banker skewed global economy, mafia run supermarkets and a European Union whose hygiene obsessed regulations have nothing to do with health but everything to do with knocking out the small farmer to clear the way for agribusiness cartels. A plan based on the Third Way can finally put paid to a government long since living in the pocket of the GM and agrichemical industry and free dear Poland from incipient slavery.

The political resistance needed for the Third Way to re-emerge will not come, this time, from the largely vacant factories and shipyards. Instead it is destined to rise up from the ancient fecund soils of rural Poland, and once it does it will become an unstoppable force rising Phoenix-like out of the ashes. Only by supporting this land based uprising can we all regain control of our destinies, freed from the merciless money machine which destroys or renders toxic all that is vital, beautiful and essential to our and our planet's well-being.

"Poland Up for Grabs" will only cease to haunt my soul once we have laid to rest the demonic forces that stand behind the top-down takeover of our lives. I didn't come to Poland only to save the wild flowers, but to help turn around the fortunes of a country that has somehow found a special place in my heart. I consider this a privilege. But I will not be at peace until this radical bottom-up process of change is well under way. And to those open hearts that are such a strong feature of Polish society are added the qualities of clarity and assertiveness without which such a change cannot succeed.

I 0

Genetically Modified Morals

'The World cannot be fed without GMO (Genetically Modified Organism) crops.' This is the mantra-like response of those who have been successfully indoctrinated by the multinational GM seed corporations into spreading their profit motivated commercial doctrine into unsuspecting regions of the world.

Currently this is most popular with academics employed by the science departments of universities whose funding is, in some degree, dependent upon the biotech industry. But it is also willingly taken up by politicians who, without doing any research or indeed any thinking of their own, use the platform provided to them by the biotech giants and repeat the corporate mantras that are designed to be easily absorbed by a largely clueless public.

The reality on the ground is very different from what is churned out by the political propaganda machine. The truth is that the world would rapidly head towards starvation should GM crops become widespread. They are at the forefront of the hi-tech industrial agriculture model that has already devastated large parts of the world with its pesticide dependent monocultures and soil depleting over-mechanisation. The patenting of GM seeds simply intensifies this process by preventing farmers from saving and replanting their seeds – a practice still essential to the welfare of farming families all over the world.

Farmers in the Philippines have stated that: "The entry of GMOs will intensify landlessness, hunger and justice." African countries have condemned Monsanto's claim that GMOs are needed to feed the hungry of the world. But this has not stopped some regions of that great continent adopting Bill Gates's 'charitable' gesture of supplying cut price GM seeds and know-how to unsuspecting leaders. In India, thousands of farmers have taken their own lives because of the failure of genetically modified crops, which they were promised would out-yield their usual varieties.

Christian Aid concluded in a report in 2002 that GM crops will cause unemployment, exacerbate Third World debt, threaten sustainable farming and damage the environment – leading to widespread famine. Even farmers in the USA, where 90 per cent of maize and soya crops are now genetically modified, have discovered that yields are falling below levels of conventional crops, unmanageable 'super weeds' are regularly appearing in their fields and herbicide requirements are increasing year by year.

In a major report issued in July 2000 entitled 'Agriculture Towards 2015/30' The FAO (Food and Agriculture Organisation of the United Nations) concluded that the world will be able to produce adequate amounts of food to sustain a predicted population of 8 billion by 2030. Their extensively researched report left GM crops out, because their contribution was not considered to be of any merit – and based its conclusions on current agricultural systems and levels of technical knowledge.

It is widely recognised by those working with farmers in the Third World that there is generally no scarcity of food being grown in these regions. The reasons for hunger are largely political, ranging from uneven food distribution, markets undercut by international food dumping, lack of land security, wars and grossly inadequate incomes.

Monsanto and similar biotech corporations are hoping that a combination of ignorance of GM technology and a readiness to accept covert bribery will enable them to sway governments into allowing patented GM seeds into all the main markets of the world. The effect of this will be the cross-contamination of indigenous and local seeds and crops with GM varieties that cannot be controlled or contained, except with highly toxic nonselective chemicals. The Monsanto Corporation has already added human growth promoting genes to pigs and then claimed that this strain of pig is patented and 'belongs to them'. Any farmer who buys these pigs then has to pay patent royalties to Monsanto. Where will all this stop?

We must all learn to resist such cynically motivated attempts to profit from the contamination and deliberate perversion of our common, irreplaceable resource base. The GMO threat to our fields and food must be placed at the top of agricultural and environmental authorities' agendas. Strong actions taken now can prevent an already critical situation running totally out of control.

Any genuine concerns for the health and welfare of others have gone out of the window because of the relentless pursuit of 'new markets', 'globalisation' and 'growth'. Therefore we need to give birth to, and maintain, a new degree of vigilance and courage to ensure that such acts of ecological violence are brought to light and to the law courts (national and international) where their perpetrators must stand trial for their acts of premeditated ecocide and destruction of human life.

Spirit of Rebellion – Rebellion of the Spirit

Over the past ten years it has been my calling to help the Polish countryside, its small farmers and the good citizens of this nation to stand up against the corporate agrichemical and genetic engineering giants. For these conglomerates seem determined to move in and transform this relatively unspoiled land into a vast experimental toxic laboratory.

Working alongside my Polish partner, Jadwiga Lopata, I have been able to draw directly upon previous experience in coming up with a plan to address the David and Goliath like struggle that has confronted us. Our 'battle' has not only been directed at the predatory corporations, but also at a complicit government and a generally unaware public.

As a practising organic farmer at a time when abandoning chemicals in favour of compost was regarded as a deeply regressive and foolish act, I had become accustomed to being shot at by posturing agricultural scientists, pharmaceutical fanatics and government lackeys who had swallowed the corporate 'party line'.

But I had been sustained throughout by the extraordinary results that greeted me as I helped my farm transition from its agrichemical-aided beginnings to a now thriving ecological unit. This, and those few passionate and creative colleagues who had embarked upon the same 'swimming against the tide' activities around the same time – kept the spirit of endeavour alive in me, while the ever demanding 'hands-on' routine of the farming calendar ensured that I remained strongly earthed.

Already in 1987 I had seen the GMO (Genetically Modified Organism) danger looming up ahead and wrote about it in the Soil Association journal at that time. By the mid 1990s the first

GM experimental research crops were being planted in the UK –
and almost instantly destroyed by a powerful alliance of activists
from various ecological organisations. So successful were such
actions that the plots were eventually wrapped-up and the supermarkets, faced by a high profile 'Frankenstein Food' campaign,
pulled any remaining GM produce off the shelves.

At this time (as I have detailed in earlier chapters), I had my
hands full leading a campaign to try to stop the British
government attempting to ban the sale of unpasteurised milk,
which just happened to be the main product of my mixed organic
farm! Somehow, with just five hundred such milk producers in
the country, we managed to beat off the government and keep
our 'Real Milk' sales going, much to the pleasure of the equally
determined consumers who still swear by such milk's amazing
efficacy and health giving properties. So by the time I passed
most of my farming operations over to a fellow organic farmer in
2000, I was well versed in the rigours of political campaigning
and grass roots activism.

What is it that gives us the will to take on our oppressors? The
enduring impetus behind such efforts seems to make its presence
known (for me) via a strong feeling of 'righteous indignation'
which wells up when faced by callous attempts to tear asunder
all that is best about life. This indignation is then channelled into
a determination not to give in, but instead to reverse all attempts
to thwart and control our creative initiatives and aspirations.

So it was in 2000 that, inspired by Jadwiga Lopata, I began to
spend large periods of time in Poland as co-director of the
International Coalition to Protect the Polish Countryside
(ICPPC). Almost at once it became apparent that Poland was
under threat from predatory GM corporations anxious to get
their genetically modified organisms into the system unnoticed
by the majority. What followed was a full-time campaign to try to
raise public and political awareness and reverse the threat.

In 2004, Poland joined the European Union. This opened the

door for a clutch of agribusiness monsters to seize their chance to get established on Polish soils; and for the GM corporations to exert an intense lobbying effort on Polish parliamentarians to allow commercial GM production into the country.

Drawing upon earlier campaign experience in the UK, I suggested that we work towards blocking off the onrush of GM products through working on a province by province basis, rather than merely lobbying the government in Warsaw. We aimed, in short, to surround the centre from the peripheries, a classic guerrilla strategy which we applied to our non-violent resistance to GMOs. Our campaign concluded eighteen months later with every one of Poland's sixteen provinces making an official self-declaration of their 'GMO Free Zone' status.

Jadwiga threw herself into this campaign with great passion. Her heart is inseparable from the rolling hills and plains of her native land. These derive their character from the patchwork of small strip farms and burgeoning wild flower meadows of traditional Polish agriculture – now under acute threat of irredeemable pollution. Jadwiga and I somehow managed to start a ball rolling and push it along until the board of each province arrived at the self-affirmative conclusion that they did not want their province's food and natural biodiversity contaminated by foreign genes and accompanying foreign corporate invaders.

In May of that same year (2006), succumbing to pressure from the provinces, the President of Poland signed a declaration to ban the import and trading of GM seeds – and Poland became the first country in Europe (if not the world) officially to ban GMO in agriculture. An extraordinary outcome! I tell this story, not through any desire to seek acclaim, but to inspire others to recognise what can be done with determination and imagination, and incidentally, only the very minimum of funds.

What gives impetus and equilibrium to carrying out such action? The starting point, in my view, is an internal feeling of rising rebellion. Rebellion against the crushing stupidity of the 'status quo'. Against the moribund imagination of those who are elected to make the policies upon which most of human life on this planet is predicated. This rising sense of deep injustice is an instinct with distinctly human origins. A kind of kick in the backside wakeup call catalysed at the deepest levels of our instinct to survive and thrive.

But it is not only a personal rebellion. It is a rebellion of the spirit itself. That is to say, it is an awakening of the spirit which is the real us, not the compromised sleep walking condition which is the pervading condition of consumer indoctrinated individuals of today, the endless stream of dumbed-down servitude which cripples human beings at the spiritual level and turns them into mechanical automata.

When the spirit itself rebels, we are on our way to experiencing what it means to be 'fully human'. To be driven by a force which does not know the meaning of the two words "I can't". Life itself speaks through us as the spirit rebels and refuses to be cordoned-off into the cul-de-sac and denial that become our weapons of phony self-protection against everything that really matters.

And what matters more than blocking all attempts to institutionalise the outright theft of our very DNA?

What matters more than laying one's self on the line to prevent the mutilation and degradation of the very gene pool upon which all planetary life depends?

The spirit rebels because it gets a message that its own Divine constitution is coming under the scalpel of some soulless form of 'science', divorced both from nature and from the subtle power of human intuition. Its own subtle essence is being loaded into the laboratory syringe, its unique and sacred character reduced to just a number on a sterile pharmaceutical production line. And we who are at one with this universal Spirit rise in rebellion along with it. And accompanying our rebellion comes a great surge of cosmic support. It is as if angels were to spring out of their routine communication roles with a largely unreceptive populous – and fly on ahead, illuminating the path on which we must travel.

You are sceptical? If so, that is only because you allow your intellectual conditioning to precede your responsive soul. Your busy mind is blocking out the poetic essence, which reflects your deepest instincts. And while you do this, the forces of darkness laugh their hollow laughter in full knowledge that their master plan remains unchallenged and unharmed. Laugh and turn the screw one more notch.

The moral is that if you sit doing nothing you will have your life taken away from you.

If millions sit doing nothing, then whole countries fall captive to the architects of control. When billions sit and do nothing, then our entire world can fall into a state of abject slavery. Look around you. Here we are.

The antidote to doing nothing is to lay oneself on the line to prevent the debasement of that which threatens the sanctity of Life. Those just surviving on $2 a day cannot be expected and are not able to engage in such actions. But those living on $100 a day surely can. Do not try to side-step this truth; you will only fall further into your own self-delusion. Embrace it and you will instantly become a receptor of the 'Angels of Good Fortune'. And the unseen forces that love our planet and love humanity will come to your aid in combating the oppressors of all that is Divine and Noble in life.

So, in the spring of 2006, Poland led the world, passing an act of parliament banning the import and trading of genetically modified seeds and plants. The country was spared the fate of the USA, Spain, Argentina, Brazil, India and others whose governments decided to allow GM plantings and the accompanying cross-contamination of natural or organic crops.

But politics being as it is, one year later this Polish government fell from power. It was replaced by a new administration with a different agenda, supported by big commerce, Big Pharma and big profits.

The struggle over the next five years, and at the time of writing, is to try to hold the line. This means campaigning to maintain the GMO Free credentials won through the hard fought campaign that led to the initial ban.

Our work at ICPPC is tough, relentless and often exasperating; but it remains an absolute necessity if we are to have any chance of developing ecological agriculture on a serious scale. Moreover, we believe that our success or failure has profound implications well beyond the borders of Poland. For only the growth of an ecologically-based agriculture can offer us any chance of maintaining a food chain free from toxic carcinogens and free from the fertility depleting GM crops, which are the agrarian counterparts to Weapons of Mass Destruction.

What are we waiting for? People across Europe, the Americas and – crucially – the emerging economies of Asia and Africa need to join in their hundreds of thousands, even their millions. We need to work together in the process of overcoming those who continue to block the arteries of life with every kind of obstructive, cunning and vile artifice, in their lust for absolute profit, power and control.

Even as the Earth rocks on its axis, the magnetosphere dilates, hurricanes devastate coastlines, mountains crumble and repression and war threaten to overwhelm all that is of value, we must stand steadfast in the passion and courage which keep the Earth – and the universe – alive. For it is indeed the fire of life – and if we put that fire out we will also be complicit in depleting the energy of the universe of which we are a part. It is a responsibility we cannot shirk.

We have no choice other than to keep alive the spirit of rebellion through responding to the rebellion of the Spirit. For this is our most intimate and honest guide and none of us can afford to ignore its call.

12

The Eternal Present: Energy and Time

Time is another of our relatively recent inventions. Time is useful in dividing absolute energy flows into abstract segments, used largely to justify financial considerations or defined work schedules. It has been both a blessing and a curse; but rather more the latter.

The celestial movement of heavenly bodies combined with the waxing and waning moon, and the sun's twenty-four hour cycle of appearance and disappearance over the eastern and western horizons, already provide the basis for a certain broad delineation of time. For the purpose of establishing a rhythm for human activity, the circadian movement of nature is probably our best guide. However, its further dissection into hours, minutes and seconds, has served the functioning of commercial life and the efficiency of largely mundane activities, far more than it has enabled us to gain a greater comprehension of our universal origins. Therefore, we tend to operate like clockwork when we could be operating like a free flowing work of art.

In essence, time does not exist. However change does. Everything 'of this world' is changing all the time. Every cell, chromosome and nucleus in our bodies is either dying or being born – at all times. Every tree is growing, decaying and being reborn again from fallen seed – at all times. Only the invisible flame of life remains constant; that which stands behind – and empowers – all temporal change. It is a flame which is imperceptible to the human eye and not easily assimilated by our rational thought process.

We have developed a bad association with the word 'change', because so much worldly change is based on actions that are superficial and largely destructive to life; whereas the deeper, nature-driven rhythms of change, are the carriers and expressions of universal harmony: we are happier immediately we get in tune with these underlying energy flows.

It is very easy to become victimised by our human-made time. We all struggle to find a way of resolving the rhythms of nature with the self-imposed demands of the time dictated working day. In attempting to do this, and by placing some sort of financial value on the passage of time, we have put the human being under a lot of unnecessary physical and mental stress. We have made our order and rhythm of life more important than the universal rhythms that regulate nature, and in the process we have forgotten that we are part of that nature.

The more complex our daily divisions of time, the more fragmented are our lives. The more fragmented are our lives, the more desperate do we become to fit all the things we wish to achieve, into the times allocated for them ... and the faster we run (or drive) in order to try and keep up with our constantly slipping self-imposed timetables. Is this the best use we can make of our time here on planet Earth? Dividing up our days in order to more efficiently organise our already overstretched, unsustainable and unrewarding lifestyles? Everybody needs to earn money, but when the process overlays our sensitivities and deeper needs with a thousand abstractions and distractions, it is surely time to call a halt and try and work out another way forward.

All these self-imposed fractional time divisions lead us into making the wrong use of time, energy and money. Relentless adherence to such schematic divisions leads us to becoming net contributors to a broader state of global imbalance and stress; leading in turn, to an utterly wasteful use of both human nervous energy as well as the terrestrial 'mined energy' required to keep it all going. The net result is translated into ever building levels of abstraction – and general fatigue to mind, body and spirit. Although hard to avoid, all 'rushing' has a knock on effect further contributing to the already over frenetic pace of life. Time appears to move faster, and we seem to have less and less of it. We should try to stop distractedly rushing around, and instead learn how to slow down, calm and centre ourselves: to "Be Here Now". Thus 'time' is brought to us rather than our always chasing after time. In this calmed state of 'being', terrestrial time fades away, and only the state of "I Am Here Now" prevails. The 'I Am' is an impersonal and metaphysical state as opposed to an egocentric and personal one. This is a recognition that, at our centre, we are universal cosmic beings (not just bread winners) deeply connected in a loving relationship with our Creator.

We can slow ourselves down, and in so doing, gain a new sense of self control. For instance, by taking even 15 minutes in each day to sit quietly, allowing oneself to "Be" – conjoined calmly with nature and the cosmos, and removed from earthly distractions. Controlled deep breathing, in conjunction with regular yoga exercises – known in India as *Asana* – provide a highly effective way of reining-in our often turbulent minds and emotions, and gaining a fresh perspective on what may appear to be intractable problems. The objective is to set in motion a whole other way of living our lives: one which transforms linear time and energy, and enables us to find lasting and deeply satisfying levels of fulfilment, coupled with a refreshed sense of direction. We can then go on to explore the rich library of writings and teachings that exist in all cultures and faiths. These will guide and encourage us to experience a greater and more all-encompassing sense of love and compassion for everything around us – ourselves included. We can start treating ourselves as true Human Beings.

A major part of 'taking control of our outer lives' involves 'taking control of our inner lives': awakening that calm, centred place of inner balance. Starting again from "Here" gives us a whole other perspective on the razzamatazz of our restless society. A perspective that makes us aware that we *can start directing our destiny, rather than allowing circumstances to direct us.* Once we are again – or for the first time – in touch with our deeper selves, we can tune into the subtle, intuitional guidance that enables us to more confidently tackle the innumerable tasks to be undertaken to heal our planet and re-energise our local communities. In this way, earthly time is transformed, and each day takes on a fresh sense of purpose and significance.

The process of confronting, head on, each road block and hurdle on this journey, and determinedly setting about overcoming them and effecting positive change, brings a constantly renewing source of energy with it. The friction involved in making the effort taps new resources.

This is a very different energy from the one we plug into to satisfy our habitual material cravings. It is a self-generated dynamic energy, wholly different in constitution from that which leads us to lean on technically generated outside energy sources for our ease and comforts. It is a transforming process, having the power to heal, rejuvenate and inspire, leading us to discover new and exciting dimensions beyond the repetitive two and three dimensional worlds which most of us take for reality.

The process can be expressed through popular traditional English phrases such as 'grasping the nettle' or 'taking the bull by the horns'. These are more than mere clichés, for they put into words our best means of gaining such inner strength and cosmic support. There is no substitute for taking action (inner and outer) – of deliberately setting forth to transform heavy, negative energies into light, positive joys.

This process can be aided by allowing the warrior spark in ourselves to be ignited – and not being afraid to join others who have already set forth to take 'direct action' to right the wrongs that otherwise distress, repress and ultimately destroy us. *When we have experienced a sense of inner empowerment, we can begin to gain true insight into what degrees of external, technically generated power we really need to sustain ourselves.*

Meanwhile, the best we can do is to act responsibly, cease wasting energy and support all efforts to cut back on obviously polluting activities. In other words, cultivate common sense, which also means a sense of our common humanity and our common purpose with the rest of nature.

13

The Human Animal

The relationship between what we call 'human' and what we call 'animal' is a powerful one. Physiologically it is recognised that there is only a tiny difference in the DNA of the higher primate species (i.e. apes and monkeys) and that of humankind. The fact is that we are animals, and animals can rightly be ascribed many of the attributes of man. For thousands of years we have existed together, sharing our food and terrain, and during this time a great bond has developed – a certain mutual affinity and respect.

We know how loving animals can be and how curative and calming is this love they so freely give. This is particularly evident in dogs, but is also true of horses, cows, pigs, cats, and all sorts of other beasts of the field and birds of the air. All these creatures also have powerful survival instincts, and will fight to the death for their existence if necessary.

The domesticated farm animal has contributed untold support to the human race over the millennia, whether as a source of meat, milk and clothing, or as a beast of labour. To this day there are millions of donkeys, horses, cows, buffaloes and oxen helping man to till his fields and sow his corn. It has been so since biblical times and long before. One of the first processed foods consumed by man was a curd cheese, which formed itself by chance, when a donkey carrying a small sack of milk across rough terrain produced just the right amount of swaying movement to cause the milk to coagulate into a basic form of cheese. This event is purported to have happened in Anatolia (modern-day Turkey) some three to four thousand years before Christ.

Farm animals also fertilise the land. Many poor soils have been brought to life by the diligent use of farmyard manures, and as ruminants' dung is added to the compost heap. The use of cow dung in building and insulating houses and huts is still widely practised in the more pastoral areas of the world, and claims of its efficiency as an insulator are widespread. Under certain specific conditions, it also has unusual healing qualities; these are recognised and applied by Ayurvedic practitioners, under an ancient practice known as 'Homa Therapy'.

There are too many positive attributes to name when it comes to describing the richness that our animal cousins bring into the world. However, a great tragedy has arisen in our shared relationship with domesticated farm animals, and a terrible injustice has been perpetrated, by consigning certain animals to fill the role of factory farm inputs and outputs, their short lives being witnessed only by the person who feeds them and the person who kills them. In other words, their lives are dominated by those men and women who press the buttons on the machines that dispense their antibiotic-laden, genetically modified food and the conveyor belt killing machine that dispatches them. Let us not call such individuals farmers. Anyone who can endure such work is more suited to working as an executioner. So soulless, perverse and debased is this system of food production, that it defies words to describe adequately the levels of insentient and callous inhumanity to which we have descended in order to have invented such animal concentration camps.

At the other end of this chain, Mr and Mrs X, walking into their favourite neon-lit, sanitised supermarket, will encounter their animal cousin as an apparently nice piece of tender chicken or pork, hygienically wrapped in cling film, and presented in a little polystyrene tray: a 'special offer', the supermarket bargain of the day. As Mr and Mrs X observe their evening meal, they are particularly interested in the price. Is there, they might ask each other, not an even cheaper broiler at another supermarket down the road? And probably there will always be a cheaper broiler somewhere, so long as human beings regard the bird as nothing more than a cheap piece of edible flesh. So long as we close ourselves off from ourselves, and from our relationship with all sentient life forms that are part and parcel of our living world and so long as we don't ask any difficult questions regarding the buying policy of our favourite chain store, our relationship with the natural world will take a destructive form.

Factory farms are the places where thousands of animals, usually pigs and chickens, are kept in vast airless, sunless sheds, with only the very minimum space in which to move. The pigs are forced to lie on concrete cubicles and the hens are imprisoned in metal cages. They live under strip lighting, kept on 18 or 24 hours a day to encourage constant eating for weight gain and continuous egg-laying. Their diet typically consists of finely ground soya beans and maize, with added prophylactic doses of antibiotics to stave off the risk of disease that such environments always attract. The antibiotics also act as a growth promoter, causing faster weight gain. The maize and soya used in most European and North American factory farm units is genetically modified and produced on vast uniform prairies whose soils have been rendered so sterile and lifeless, that plants can grow on them only with the help of agrichemicals.

The pigs and broiler hens have frighteningly short lives – if indeed you can call their time on earth 'life'. The broilers (hens reared for meat) may make 2 months before slaughter, the pigs around three and a half months. The laying hens are as useful as their laying ability, which is encouraged by a diet of high protein soya, with added medication to keep from being struck down with disease. Into this feed are added special synthetic colours to make the yolks turn an appealing orange colour. If these colours were not added, the yolks would be pale grey, and no one would eat them. The typical life span of these birds is three months.

I have kept free range hens on my farm. Their homes being movable wooden houses, with fifty hens in each house, poles to perch on, and constant daytime access to green grass fields. Their diet of cracked wheat and whatever they forage off the land enables them to continue steady but unspectacular egg production for three to four years. Their pale orange yolks are formed by the green matter they eat as part of their natural outdoor foraging.

I have also kept outdoor, free range pigs. They root around in the earth with their snouts, and wander contentedly where they will within the confines of the field – and also sometimes the neighbour's! They can live this way for many years, the sows producing many litters of healthy piglets. The extra food they receive being a blend of home produced cereals and vegetable wastes.

There are many farms that rear their animals on systems approximately halfway between the two described here; trying to find a balance between earning a reasonable return on their investment, while managing to keep up good standards of animal welfare. These are not factory farms, just sensibly run family farming enterprises, whose financial survival is under intense pressure because the mass production factory farms undercut the market for their produce.

But it is the supermarkets that call the tune. They demand large quantities of uniform eggs and meat, regularly supplied and at precise dates. They like to deal with a few very large suppliers. Suppliers that keep 30,000 hens in one vast shed without exposure to daylight or 3,000 pigs in similarly confined conditions. The supermarkets are ruthless in their determination to get their products very cheap, so Mr and Mrs X can get their 'bargain'. The only way the producer can meet the rock bottom prices on offer, is by finding ways of raising their animals – and lots of them – at equally rock bottom costs.

Mass production factory farming has, up till now, been presented as the only way the producer can make a profit based on the unacceptably low price on offer. So Mr and Mrs X – and all other thoughtless consumers – it is you who are giving the supermarkets the perfect excuse to encourage the animal rearing methods of the factory farms, rather than the methods utilised by organic and good traditional farmers. Your insistent demand for impossibly cheap meat and the 'special bargain', drives the factory farm conveyor belt and gives credibility to systems that have no credibility in terms of human and animal dignity. I have not mentioned milk production. It would take another book to tell the whole story and others have done this already.

Animal and human can, and should, serve each other. But we have an absolute responsibility to cease mercilessly exploiting our cousins for our own greed and short sighted self-satisfaction. Once aware of the plight of such mass produced sentient birds and animals, it amounts to a criminal act to insist on continuing to purchase them. If one is buying on price – because no other meat seems affordable, it is better to eat such food much less frequently, and then try to source humanely reared, better quality meat.

There is nothing more rewarding than to raise animals and crops to a quality, standard and price that gives satisfaction to all concerned. Farmers are stewards of the land and also its trustees. Their role puts them in the position of being guardians of the quality of life in all aspects of their farms, but outstandingly so for the animals in their care, whom they come to see as a sort of extended family.

For a good farmer, the animals' health and welfare always takes precedence over financial considerations. His or her pride and humanity is at stake around the clock; and tragically, many a farmer would rather take his or her own life than see their farm fall into disrepute or insolvency. The result of insolvency is purchase of the farm by the bank from which the farmers borrowed the investment money to set up a working business, so that the farmers end up working for the bank rather than themselves or their local community. Between themselves, many farmers talk of making money and of the productive qualities of their animals and soils. But privately, most nurture soft hearts and a great love of the way of life, however tough.

We live in a time of unprecedented disconnection between town and country, and of deep misunderstanding and ignorance. This has enabled corporations, greedy for profit, to exploit the resulting lack of discernment amongst a large body of consumers. The wound this has caused is deep, and our farm animals have been especially vulnerable. But now is the time to heal these wounds. *Now* is always the best time to mend things, and newly acquired awareness must be followed by action to bring about positive change. The formula for this change lies in kindling some warmth in our hearts, then listening to – and acting on – the voice of our conscience.

Animal and human/human and animal, travel together on the path of life. We are travelling companions. But we humans have the power to organise our domesticated animals for our own ends. So if our own ends are broadly compassionate, we will give them as good a life as we are able, and they will reward us equally. This is the path of non-exploitation and balanced relationships. If we participate knowingly in using our consumer power to support animal concentration camps, we ultimately kill both the animal and the human in ourselves.

14

Health, Balance and the Life Force

What is health? Some may say 'the absence of disease', but clearly this falls far wide of the mark. A state of well-being? Certainly, but let us say more: an overall state of dynamic balance in mind, body and spirit. Universal health is expressed as an overall state of dynamic balance throughout the universe.

But what is 'dynamic balance'?

'Balance' is expressed as a pivotal point between two extremes. It is a dynamic, resonant and 'centred' state of Being. One might also describe it as 'pure economy of movement'.

At the cosmic level, the 'equilibrium of balance' comes about as a result of electro magnetically charged particles emerging in a pivotal position between the energetic forces of attraction and repulsion. Equilibrium (health) is the light energy emerging out of the friction generated by these two forces. It (health) is an uninhibited energy that radiates both inwards and outwards simultaneously. It radiates out in all directions at once, producing a gently glowing incandescence.

We on Earth are part of this dynamic universal energy and we are aspiring participants in the universal quest to find this state of true balance, true equilibrium: a state of enlightenment (being 'lit up').

That is to say, we share with the great cosmic spirit, or spirits, the desire to realise that which is our potentiality: *to realise ourselves fully*. This is the drama of life's journey; it is at once our starting point and our ultimate goal. At the quivering 'pivotal point' of equilibrium, there is no difference between the Alpha and Omega points, they are subsumed into one vibrant ever-present entity.

For us, this life journey is not just a straight line between A and B. It is more what the poet William Blake called "the crooked road of genius". In fact, there can be no straight line in our universe – everything, as Einstein and others have observed, is on a curve. Even light energy bends its way around the planets as it makes its way to Earth.

'Roundness' is the shape of our world, the planets and the great universal design of which we are all a part. It is also in the nature of energy to oscillate as it travels – a 'wave' movement – recognised, and intensely studied, by the quantum physicists in their probing of the behaviour of the minutest visible levels of matter. Ultimately, these minute particles of energy/matter were observed to transform themselves between specks of matter, waves, and what was described as 'a dance'.

The descriptions of the sub atomic particles participating in 'a dance' was a rather remarkable scientific 'discovery' – and expresses the overlap between the highest forms of scientific and artistic creativity. And that is surely the essence of it all: we are but one special expression of a shared cosmic energy. We are born in the image of our Creator, thus we share with our Creator the conscious and on-going exploration – and realisation – of all potential contained within us. *Thus the true expression of health is to be found in a manifestation of our oneness with balanced universal energies.*

What is disease?

The literal meaning of a state of 'dis-ease' is a state of 'not being at ease'! When we are not at ease with ourselves (and with our Creator), then we are out of balance. When we are out of balance, we experience anxiety, stress and depression. Essentially, we are 'not at ease with ourselves' when cut off from, or out of tune with, the dynamic of universal energy, as described above.

Such a condition expresses itself physically, as a malfunctioning of various organs of the body. Typically, this means the heart and lungs, as well the dispersal organs, including kidneys and liver. On the mental plane, it is expressed as a malfunctioning of psychic equilibrium.

It is very helpful that the word 'dis-ease' so clearly gets to the quick of the matter. Being 'at ease' suggests being in harmony with the rhythm and flow of a greater macro-cosmic energy. Not surprisingly, today, many are in search of this mysterious universal rhythm, finding in it a direct counterbalance to the fragmented and often stress laden lifestyles so many have felt impelled to adopt. Yet to be at ease for anything other than ephemeral bursts involves a significant effort and ultimately, a substantial reward. It involves changing our way of life, and helping to change the way of life around us. It involves more inner fire and less unbridled ego; more spirit and less materialism; more introspection and less arrogance. It is a journey we all must embark upon if we are to realise 'true health' and if we are to minimise the state of disease: in ourselves, in our environment, and in our society as a whole.

So when we are concerned about human health, we should always first set that concern in the macro-cosmic, universal context – from where it originated. The problem is that in the majority of cases we don't. We are primarily concerned about ourselves – seen as divorced and separate from nature and the greater whole. This means that we are already starting from a position of 'disequilibrium' – and in this situation it is only possible to speak about preventing or curing one *particular* illness or unhealthy trait, within a greater sphere of overall sickness.

In medical terms, this is largely the role played by allopathic medicine, which has (in some cases) been remarkably efficient in this two-dimensional approach to treatment. Symptoms emerge, illness strikes, and a solution to reducing and/or removing that illness is often found. This has been particularly true in treating the rampant spread of certain viral diseases.

But this is not always so of course. Pathogens become increasingly sophisticated in their ability to overcome medicines, just as bugs become immune to pesticides in agriculture, and the cat and mouse game between disease and cure continues indefinitely.

This might be considered an almost acceptable resolution, if it were not for the fact that the human body takes a hit each time such medicines are dispensed. This is because their composition incorporates synthetic elements that, while helping to eradicate the particular problem they are designed to deal with, load other areas of the body with an excess of chemical components that put stress on the organs that must in turn try to deal with them. These medicines, after excretion, ultimately land up in the environment, causing pollution of ground water, soils, streams and rivers. They are known to have caused fish to change sex and to promote algae that smother oxygen. There is a growing danger that medical components can also get into our drinking water supplies, ensuring a potentially lethal cocktail of unwanted chemical medicines in our daily diet.

Allopathic medicine's main weakness is to be found in its reticence to treat the underlying causes of disease – rather than just its end manifestation. There is an analogy here with the farmer who relies on agrochemical pesticides to suppress disease in his unsustainably managed fields. Driving the vast pharmaceutical empires that most allopathic doctors cherry pick from to prescribe quick fixes to their patient's complaints, are a few powerfully placed individuals, intent upon controlling society's dietary habits for their own ends. An intrinsic part of this strategy is to make individuals parasitically dependent upon purchasing the patented 'cures' that they offer. In other words, to keep society just sick enough to enable the coffers of 'Pharma Ltd' to be continuously replenished.

As part of our daily diet, every food additive, colour, preservative and flavour enhancer, is a tool for polluting and clogging up the arteries of natural good health. All 'long shelf life' processing aids contribute to the steady evolution of 'Synthetic

Man'. With the addition of genetically modified food, it has now been scientifically proven that the GM traits pass on into the human gut once ingested, altering our very DNA and turning us into a new species: genetically modified Homo sapiens. In addition, with 'Big Pharma' owned and synthesised transgenic medicines and patented pseudo-vaccinations, it will soon be quite possible to legitimately ask the question "Who owns our genes?"

All 'agribusiness' hybridisation and engineering of the indigenous seeds that once formed the secure foundation of our diets will inevitably destroy key components of the subtle living energies that are so vital to positive health. *In the rush for 'quantity' and 'profit' rather than 'quality' and 'health', the living nutritional values of foods have greatly suffered. Society at large has become the experimental laboratory for an increasingly synthetic dietary regime never before ingested by humankind.*

This is further evidenced by all those chemical-rich, synthetic vitamins and 'virtual' supplements that line the groaning shelves of many so called 'health stores'. The daily consumption of such pills adds yet another synthesised chemical component to our already polluted bodies and, by extension, to our minds. Such pills are a false substitute for the real plants and minerals, even in crushed form, provided to us directly by nature, especially those that are nurtured along ecological principles or merely growing in the wild.

The only things to be kept healthy by 'medic-business' mass pill production, are the bank balances of the pharmaceutical giants that succeed in maintaining 'control' over our lives – leaving us basically 'out of control'. By and large, it seems, our health is largely in the hands of those who profit by our illness. We are, in effect, dumbed down by retaining our unquestioned dependency upon the products of such regimes. Our subtle metabolism, creative thinking processes and natural joie de vivre have the vital edge taken off them by synthetic cures – and likewise our judgement and independence is also curtailed. Taken a little further, we can soon fail to even retain sufficiently sharp critical faculties to discern the source of our malaise, repression and depression. We are then truly victims of the system: corporate globalised 'health care' as laid out by the 'Codex Alimentarius' committee and the World Health Organisation and put into practice by the drug and commodity barons of this exploited world.

However, within the world of formalised medicines there is hope; more humane, caring, time honoured and beneficial treatments do manage to push their heads above the parapet! Homeopathic treatments (for example) situate themselves closer to the macrocosmic, universal health reality. They do this by treating the 'whole person', seeing in her or him a complex interconnected dynamic composed of hundreds of inherently related elements all reacting and inter-reacting with each other at all times.

Ayurvedic (Indian) and Chinese practices are also founded in this 'whole person' analysis and care approach. Both demonstrate a highly sophisticated, age old, yet somehow absolutely contemporary understanding of the subtle vibratory levels that pervade our human condition. They use herbal and mineral components in their treatments that have no adverse side-effects on the human body or wider environment.

Such approaches also take into account mental and psychic states: mind as well as body. Psychologists and psychiatrists are trained to 'heal the psyche', but this still only represents one component of our overall health. Let me quote a short excerpt from a book by Maya Tiwari entitled 'Ayurveda Secrets of Healing':

Three primordial forces, or principles, interweaving to create five elements – space, air, fire, water, earth – give birth to the entirety of creation. The principle of stillness, 'tamas', replenishes the universe and its being and is the main principle and support within the physical universe and human life. The principle of harmonic and cosmic intelligence, 'sattva', maintains universal and individual stasis and awareness.

The three cosmic principles, called 'gunas' operating through the five elements they have created, directly inter-phase with human existence.

The other *guna*, not mentioned in the quotation above, is *Rajas*, the principle of movement and creativity, which balances the principle of *tamas*, much as in traditional Chinese thought the active, dynamic Yang balances the receptive Yin.

I do not mean to convey the message that western medicine's more specialist approach is wholly misguided, as this would be a simplistic interpretation. However allopathic medicine only finds meaning as a last resort remedy, as one remedial tool within the greater medical tool box. In its failure to look at the whole person, western medicine misses the universal health bigger picture, which is essential for maintaining the long term health of body, mind and spirit.

But it is outside the realm of professional medical knowledge that the most widespread variety of health promoting formulae exists. At the grass roots, informal level, every culture in the world has a great storehouse of tried and tested treatments. Such treatments very closely correlated with the native plants, herbs, trees and minerals that make up the local habitat. Tens of thousands of combinations, concoctions and potions are utilised, drawing from a native wisdom going back hundreds, if not thousands, of years. The world's peasant farmers retain a great storehouse of knowledge of the attributes of these precious herbs, plants, trees and even minerals. They are the last guardians of our 'managed' nature-sourced medicinal heritage.

Such cures are intimately connected with the intricate biodi-versity of each region. Lose the biodiversity, and one loses the means of healing – and we are on the verge of such a loss. A rich foundation of flora and fauna is at the root of widespread good health; and we are the primary mangers of this biodiversity and main recipients of its bounty. *It is our responsibility – and nobody else's – to ensure the vital balance of all flora, fauna and soils on our planet. Even if this means leaving alone certain wildernesses – such as the world's rain forests – that are an abundant source of as yet unrecognised flora and a vast storehouse of potential cures to the illnesses that continue to ravage our planet.*

Mismanagement, exploitation without giving back in return; pollution, and a general 'couldn't care less' attitude, constitute crassly bad practice, and a shameful refusal to recognise our wider universal responsibilities to look after and nurture good health in all that is precious. Negative and cynical thinking is itself a disease, as well as an invasive pollutant. Everything good in life stems from the effort to take a positive and caring attitude – and trying to encourage the same in others.

Microcosm and macrocosm are two parts of one whole. A small cosmos: our planet and biosphere – and a big cosmos: our universe and beyond, reflect each other. If the earth is made sick by our bad habits, so will the greater universe of which the earth is a part, take on a part of that sickness. If the universe becomes sick, so will the earth and so will man. *We are subject to the law of cause and effect and cannot break out of this 'bounce' unless, and until, the laws of man harmonise with universal laws.* It is supposed to be the purpose of universities ('universe-ities') to teach this, and it should be the primary role of our hospital service to practise it.

We will only cure ourselves, our planet and our universe, through recognising our inseparable mutual interdependence, and by accompanying this recognition with consistent good practice and good discipline. This way we will discover 'Health' – perhaps for the first time.

Resolutions:

Starting at the local and regional level:

1. Find best practitioners with good knowledge of herbal health cures, and where to find best wild and cultivated plants and minerals.
2. Start local clinics based on the application of this knowledge
3. Attract trained doctors with awareness of how to treat the 'whole person' – holistic medicine. Also homeopathic, Ayurvedic and Chinese skills.
4. Draw in a local GP seeking to widen his/her field of knowledge. Encourage good communication between allopathic and holistic healers.
5. Raise the health awareness of the community in line with the points raised in this chapter.
6. Build awareness concerning the superior nutritional and health-giving values of local, fresh, flavourful and seasonal, ecologically raised foods. Remember: when it comes to illness, prevention is better than cure.
7. Ensure all local drinking water is of the highest achievable quality.
8. Ensure that spiritual sensitivities are respected and built upon.
9. Find a good balance between physically and mentally demanding activities and genuine relaxation. Fresh air, exercise and a positive frame of mind, form the time honoured foundation of basic physical and mental health.
10. Build into all human relationships awareness, respect and compassion.
11. Completely redesign hospitals to be places of beauty, peace and tranquillity; and make holistic as well as allopathic treatments available for all patients.
12. Ensure that hospitals are supplied with good quality fresh foods and that in-house catering enhances their nutritional values.

15

European "Super-State" – One Step Closer or Imminent Collapse?

Jean Monnet, the founding father of the European Union, had a very particular vision of Europe's future back in 1952, and he expressed it in a letter to a colleague on 30th April that year:

> Europe's nations should be guided towards the super-state without their people understanding what is happening. This can be accomplished by successive steps, each disguised as having an economic purpose, but which will eventually and irreversibly lead to federation.

Here, in a nutshell, we plainly see the trickery that stands behind the fabricated 'Union' of individual nations, each of which was led to believe that its economic and social stability would prosper once it committed to the 'common market' and the various treaties which mark its inexorable passage to 'super-state'. The actual mission of the founders of the EU has always been something of a chimera; Monnet's letter makes it clear however, that the motivation was both idealistic and elitist. The supranational entity was to be created "without (their) people understanding what was happening" following a pattern of elitist, oligarchical ambition stretching back through past dynasties.

We can trace the roots of this latest 'super-state' experiment to the Schuman Plan of 1951, which was signed up to by six countries and took the form of the Treaty of Paris centred around coal and steel industries being placed under common management, ostensibly to prevent any recurrence of the death and destruction of the Second World War. Germany, France,

Italy, the Netherlands, Belgium and Luxembourg were the signatories to this treaty whose stated aim was to ensure that none of these countries could ever again manufacture weapons of war to be used against the other.

Then in 1957, the same six countries expanded cooperation to other economic sectors and signed The Treaty of Rome. Thus the 'European Economic Community', also known as The Common Market, came into being. The UK joined this in 1973 under then Prime Minister Edward Heath. The formal creation of the European Union, under the guidance of Jacques Delors, did not occur until February 1992 under the Maastricht Treaty. It formalised the introduction of the European Parliament and European Commission, the latter gaining considerable 'management power' under Jacques Santer, its first president. Interestingly the Commission was originally to be named "The High Authority", which has strongly Masonic overtones. But this name was dropped in the 1960s. The single currency (Euro) element of the expanding Union was launched in 1999, along with the European Central Bank. Lastly, the Lisbon Treaty of December 2009 created the new post of President of the European Council.

Within this brief synopsis of the EU's birth and expansion, we can detect the process of creeping homogenisation which reflects Jean Monnet's covert master plan. As intended, on the surface it certainly appears that economic considerations were to the fore, notwithstanding the supposedly benign 'common' interests like modernised infrastructure, the Common Agricultural Policy and the 'no border' agreements which were deemed to give the EU a more flowing socio-economic (and cultural) connectivity. The Common Agricultural Policy (CAP) was supposed to ensure that no one would go hungry in the new Europe and that farming interests would be financially protected against undue volatility within the wider market. Needless to say, the subsidised monocrops and intensive livestock holdings of the CAP have proved an unmitigated disaster for traditional biodiverse mixed family farms, food quality and the ecology of European farmland. Distorted (subsidised) trading policies have also exacted their toll on others.

What is undeniable in all this, is that Monnet's grand experiment has concentrated a very large amount of power into very few hands; and those hands are a long way removed from the hands of the labourers and workers who continue to form the majority of European Union citizens. The creation of the single currency (Eurozone) has served to expose the fault lines that have, on more than one occasion, come to the surface of EU affairs. Whatever the founding fathers may have thought, the idea that countries as socially, culturally and economically contrasting as Greece and Germany, could find commonality via some form of 'fiscal agreement' was anything but wise.

The creation of the European Central Bank epitomises the 'trading block' mentality of the Eurozone. It has, as Winston Churchill once noted, brought home the fact that the EU could operate like "A United States of Europe". A United States of Europe is just what Europe is becoming, with the President of the European Commission acting as the front man, a powerful Central Bank acting as Europe's vault and a weak parliament struggling to introduce some semblance of democracy.

Within this top heavy and highly bureaucratic regime, global banking cartels have fully exploited the underlying sense of political insecurity. The European Central bank has teamed up with the International Monetary Fund to act as central controllers of the destinies of struggling Eurozone countries. The result is a cold and soulless brand of exploitation which appears blind to anything other than the imposition of bureaucratic-authoritarian control structures that suck dry the assets of any country foolish enough to seek its financial support.

After presiding over the collapse of various European economies, Jose Manuel Barroso has used his position as

President of the European Commission to recommend the imposition of a European super-state as the only effective medicine left to hold the troubled 'Union' together. Resistance to this solution is taken as a negation of the spirit of the project and those who dare to raise their voices as 'deniers'. Sixty years on from the date of the Monnet letter and the framework of the envisioned super-state is pushed into place.

As ailing Eurozone member states pledge their dwindling national assets to the voracious demands of the IMF and ECB, the interest payments that the IMF and ECB exact continue to fuel the financier led cabal's war chest. Countries outside the Eurozone are now being asked to further top-up this chest, because apparently there is not enough in it to prepare further poisoned loan packages for the next victims.

What Jean Monnet had in mind when he wrote his infamous letter, was the carefully crafted, covert instigation of an ultimate power heist. The aim was to install, permanently, a small band of all powerful technocrats and oligarchs in the undisputed driving seat of one of the largest trading blocks of the planet. Under this regime, the sovereignty of nation states becomes strategically weakened and so heavily dependent upon outside economic support that it ultimately ceases to operate as a functional 'sovereign' system. Decisions of national importance once made via elected parliaments, are usurped by the centralised control system based in Brussels, but directly linked to London, New York, Washington, Frankfurt, Paris, Rome and Tokyo.

Any country not part of this 'club' automatically becomes sidelined as a second class nation with little or no right to sit on key committees and influence the future. The fiscal union club is held up as the Holy Grail by which all nations must abide if they are to be members of the inner sanctum. Under this regime transnational corporations, bankers and EU bureaucrats flourish, while the working citizens of the EU are imprisoned in a modern serfdom in which the banker controlled European Commission and signed-up nation states demand that the European labour force bail out the private banks by accepting lower pay, later retirement and the loss of social services.

In this way, we (the people) are asked to carry the can and submit to the austerity measures imposed upon us in order that governments can bail out banks and banks can satisfy their Eurocrat pay masters ensconced behind their mahogany desks at the European Financial Stability agency. In close proximity also sit the shadowy 'Frankfurt Group'. According to Larry Elliot, economics correspondent of the Guardian, the Frankfurt group is:

an unelected cabal made up of eight people: (2012) Christine Lagarde (IMF);Angela Merkel; Francois Hollande; Mario Draghi (president of ECB); Jose Manuel Barroso (president European Commission); Jean Claude Juncker (chairman Eurogroup); Herman van Rompuy (president European Council) and Olli Rehn (Europe's Economic and Monetary affairs commissioner). This group, which is accountable to no one, calls the shots in Europe.

Given the free rein which this cabal now exercises in its management of European (if not global) financial matters, it's hardly surprising that *money and power* constitute the overriding theme of Eurozone ambitions. How many times have you heard, over the past few months, heads of state declaring that meetings must be concluded at such and such a time "in order to give the markets a clear message." Please note: not the people – but *the markets*. Everything, it now seems, is beholden to 'the markets'. They have become a totem to which we are all expected to bow our heads in obeisance. The pervasive consumption and growth ideology and the covert lust for power which accompanies its pre-eminence suggest a deep sickness reaching into the heart of society. It is a sickness which gives licence to the establishment of technocratic dictatorships and the demotion of the instinct for democracy.

Jean Monnet no doubt recognised this at the inception of the European Union. Maybe he saw how a small group of well-schooled power seekers would be able to engineer the economic collapse of countries that failed to fulfil the diktats of the private club which he and his colleagues had instigated. Was it foreseen that it might be possible to achieve what the Reichstag had failed to achieve, but this time with little or no need for bloodshed?

In any event, gone is the Europe standing for a group of independent nation states banding together when appropriate, on internationally significant issues. The entire edifice of the extended family of nations called Europe, has been brought to a point of crisis due to the artifice and brinkmanship of the executors of this global power grab. The result is a centralised power that now controls much of the media, the politicians, the market and the people. "We give them what we make them think they want" is an apt summary of the heist's blue print for success. In a world of mass media hype (virtual reality, 'shopping' as the number one leisure pursuit, plus every conceivable gismo to play around with), one can see how the artful creation of these superficial distractions has combined to become such a powerful opiate.

Tragically, the bankrupt materialistic imagination of the modern European fails to penetrate the veil of deceit which has allowed the clandestine take-over to proceed so smoothly. As Aldous Huxley warned in *Brave New World Revisited* (1958): "Democracy and Freedom will be the theme of every broadcast and editorial. Meanwhile the ruling oligarchy and its highly trained elite soldiers, police, thought-manufacturers and mind manipulators will quietly run the show as they see fit."

So here we stand, on the edge of the precipice, yet mostly failing to recognise that it is a precipice. The federal super-state, currently managed by the infamous 'troika', is closing around us, regardless of any nation's membership or non-membership of the single currency regime. This control system works on the principle of keeping people just intelligent enough to serve the system but not intelligent enough to recognise that *it is* a system. It has been largely successful in this mission, since up until now we have been pacified into accepting the role of grudging servitude with few signs of outward resistance.

However, all that may be about to change. Signs of rebellion are appearing where once only the mists of sleep prevailed. The extremity of US and EU neo colonial war-mongering in Africa, the Persian Gulf and Central Asia, is raising eyebrows and not a few hairs on the nape of the necks of many, including those who were once broadly sympathetic to the direction of policy. Oil companies are turning in record profits; banks are barely humbled by their carefree profligacy of 2008/9 and multi-millionaires are created every week in extravagant game shows and lottery draws. All this while government instigated 'austerity' packages are bearing down on citizens struggling to make a reasonable living and hold onto some modicum of social responsibility and decorum. Something has to give; and probably more than Greece, Ireland and Portugal.

Our long running pretence at being anything other than a schizoid and hypocritical society is finally falling away. The bare bones of the truth can no longer be disguised behind placatory rhetoric and artful deception. As the realisation of what stands in front of us grows, we have a very real choice to make: stand on our own two feet and free ourselves from the encircling tentacles of the Monnet and Delors inspired supra-national dictatorship. The alternative is to slide further under its control – losing our ability to forge our destinies for generations to come. The choice has never been so stark. It is surely down to each of us to reach into richer soils and ensure that something altogether better is brought into being

What might a sensible alternative look like? In mapping out a future strategy, the phrase 'reversion to the local' should become crucial. No thoughtful individual is likely to desist from the belief that some form of central committee is necessary to ensure the effective management of a country. However, the constant stream of abuse of power in high places is undoubtedly forcing us to reconsider just what sort of criteria is needed for a new template, so that good, thoughtful, honest citizens take up and/or become elected to office so as to restore power to local communities or nation states.

When one considers the European situation as a whole, it becomes apparent that an area as culturally and geographically diverse as Europe needs to be cared for by those who best understand the unique social, cultural and economic patterns that exist in each region. This would rule out a distant centralised bureaucracy trying to manipulate events on a scale that renders such a task impossible even if the most sympathetic souls are in charge. It points instead to regional, self-governing entities establishing themselves as the main administrative centres; bodies able to best nurture and care for the social and physical resource base of each region and answer to the needs of those who reside within this region.

I do not necessarily regard the traditional model of 'parliamentary democracy' as the only model worth considering here. The Swiss example of locally based direct or plebiscitary democracy might well be worth considering in many other regions of Europe. There should be a trawl for the best and most wise heads when looking for the most appropriate human talent to serve on a regional administrative body. Certainly any 'big egos' must be out of the running. A key criterion in establishing a largely peaceful and well balanced community is to keep the scale small. Over and over again it has been seen that once a cohesive community is enlarged beyond its ability to be largely self-sustaining, it staggers and falls, wreaking much destruction along the way.

Therefore, it follows that many self-managing small communities, each interconnecting with the other at a grass roots level, ultimately make for a more cohesive and coherent overall picture than that achieved by one centralised command centre trying to impose a policy upon all citizens.

For example, small communities can and should devise their own economic policies, housing needs and power and food distribution systems – for a start. People need to feel the security that comes with being identified with a geographical location which looks after its own basic needs and the needs of others within an easily identifiable extended family.

This is not to say that some form of central body is not necessary – it is. But its tasks should be limited to international and macro-economic concerns, defence issues, some (but not all) policing, long distance transportation and immigration. A central body is also needed to act as an overseer and coordinator of proper cooperation between the regions.

Every entity in this Universe balances internal against external energies; the friction produced is what creates 'balance' and the gravitational field that binds the universe into one great body. One great body composed of millions of unique parts. Why should it be any different on Earth?

The Europe that most of us probably yearn for would draw on its traditional roots once more, but add to this a dynamic vision that ensures a closing of the income and entitlement gap that provokes such a blatant imbalance between what is termed 'standards of living'. What is needed is putting in place a cooperative based socio-economic vision that gives people less reason or opportunity to attack and demean each other because they are working for the same identifiable ends.

The nation state remains better than a totalitarian technocracy – that's for sure. But the nation state, in most cases, is too static and complacent an institution to cope with the extreme upheavals we are likely to face in the years ahead. True leadership comes from 'practicing what one preaches' and this requires an approach inspired by Mahatma Gandhi's philosophy, based on principled, non-exploitative leadership by example that is easily recognised by decent people and does not try to exploit them.

The essential point is that if people are going to be encouraged to take control over their destinies they must also recognise that this involves taking part in the shared management of the greater community of which they are a part. When no responsibility is taken, which is typical today, it is because of a residual belief that someone else in some anonymous office building in some concrete jungle is going to make that decision for one. That is the source of the rapidly accelerating decay of the 'democratic experiment' of which we are a part.

16

You Can't Eat Gold

The great rush to find a safe haven for financial investments has led many supposedly savvy citizens, to put their money into gold. This has caused the value of the precious metal to soar, touching $1,800 an ounce at the time of writing, giving investors a sense of security that their money is safe and likely to hold its value.

However, in a world undergoing seismic socio-economic and environmental convulsions that are growing by the day, gold may not prove to be the solution to our future security that many are hoping for.

If one stands back a little from the spinning vortex of speculative financial roulette that preoccupies the world's media and many of her better-off citizens, one will observe that unfortunately gold is inedible (some will say 'fortunately') and is less easy to turn into ploughshares than other baser metals. This fact has not gone unnoticed by globally oriented financial investors. These speculators have recently started pouring money into agricultural land holdings as a hedge against higher food prices, set against a guaranteed demand for world staples like wheat, rice, maize and sorghum. Unfortunately the objectives of such investment policies are not benign, but rather are symptomatic of the same convulsive profit driven motives that have served as a catalyst for the seismic economic swings of the past decade.

So, where do we turn when all around is turmoil stirred by inflated egos, unashamed greed and rabid exploitation?

To find an answer to this conundrum, we should start with a careful consideration of the circumstances that have brought us to this point. Then, we might move forward to a plan of action which offers a longer term commitment to a saner and perhaps 'simpler' model of everyday living – one which shifts us decisively away from the present day capitalist consumerist ethos that has brought our planet to the brink of asset-stripped ecocide and unchecked human inequality.

In seeking to raise our awareness of the background to this unprecedented upheaval, it soon becomes apparent that there is some other force operating behind the front line villains picked out as being responsible for the rising and falling fortunes of the global economy. Those 'in the news' are often simply puppets of this unseen shadow regime which appears to be intent upon a far going domination of global events for its own ends.

The regime appears to be composed of a small group of very wealthy individuals and corporations that have established a controlling influence over both national government and the international financial institutions that form the lynchpin of the global economy. It is a mostly shadowy cartel whose field of influence includes such institutions as the Bilderbergers, The Trilateral Commission, The World Bank, The International Monetary Fund, The World Trade Organisation, The European Central Bank and the Federal Reserve of the USA. Its leaders are also strategically placed to control events within the European Union, the North American Free Trade Association (NAFTA) and the Pacific Rim economic zone.

Banking empires, pharmaceutical giants, oil magnates and food and seed monopolies are well represented within this club, which exercises decisive control over all our lives without us ever really noticing it. At their behest, moral codes and human values are flouted with reckless abandon, while brutal wars are started in foreign countries with almost complete impunity. It is as if the fascist regimes of the World War II era did not end with the Nuremberg trials, for many of their attitudes and even practices have re-established a formidable foothold within Western and North American society. Democracy, in this context, becomes increasingly a façade for corporate intrigue and the 'National

Security State', with the parties of 'left' and 'right' offering little or no genuine choice.

Recognising this state of affairs for the first time can be a shock, especially if one has pinned one's faith in the status quo to see us through these "troubled times". However, reality it is, and once we have absorbed the truth there can be no turning back. Which brings us once again to the question: "Where does one turn when all around is turmoil?"

The answer is – first we have to turn to ourselves; to recognise that we are complicit in allowing such a dark agenda to have become adopted right in our midst. After all, it is we ourselves who have repeatedly put our faith in increasingly autocratic rulers who freely exercise the levers of despotic power. It is we ourselves who have handed responsibility to run our affairs to those who are masters of spin, deception and propaganda. It is we who have filled the role that British Prime Minister Neville Chamberlain filled on the cusp of World War II when he held up a scrap of paper and declared it to contain Hitler's promise that Nazi Germany would never invade the United Kingdom. We too, like Chamberlain, have ourselves acted as 'appeasers' in subordinating our destinies to the diktats of the corporate vandals and the smiling politicians in their pay.

We have freely allowed ourselves to be duped into a state of virtual paralysis by a corporate media whose agenda has nothing to do with "raising awareness" but a great deal to do with keeping us busy with the trappings of superficial consumerism, 'reality' shows and endless light entertainment. Together, the mainstream media have become a vast propaganda machine that pumps out the relentless message that we should strive ceaselessly to acquire the means to purchase our pleasures from the glittering shelves of the global market place.

That said, these shelves are now beginning to lose their lustre and the scales are beginning to fall from our eyes. We can begin to see that we confused this 'virtual reality' with actual reality.

The world turns out not to be a hypermarket after all, but a sentient being in an advanced stage of severe fever; poisoned, polluted and exploited almost beyond recognition – by us – the trolley-pushing, brand-seeking puppets. We are the puppets of a global corporate elite, that small cartel marching on its robotic way to the grand takeover of every last bankable asset on planet earth, as well as all those who, consciously or unconsciously, submit to becoming pawns in its sinister master plan.

But now it's time to take back our power and to take firm control of our destinies. We can still make this choice – it's not too late. Nobody with the means of survival needs to be a slave – and nobody with any portion of land need go without food. We are fast becoming aware that 'money in the bank' is no guarantee of our future security. As dying state and private financial institutions increasingly empower themselves to reach ever deeper into our pockets, we struggle to grasp the fact that much of what they steal goes straight into the pay cheque of the brightest scavengers and the bonuses of already bloated bosses. We barely seem to notice when our revenue payments are used to crank up still further the deadly imperialist war machine so that it can bludgeon its way through yet more oil and mineral-rich countries in order to fulfil insatiable material addictions and barely disguised neo-colonial ambitions.

However, behind all events is a law of karma which states "for every action there is an equal and opposite reaction." And just as the despotic forces of imperialism appear to be wresting decisive control over humankind, strong voices of reason and truth are rising to challenge its dominion. Right in amongst the genocidal acts of nefarious despots we are witnessing the dawning of fresh visions of another way mankind can look after itself and this sentient planet upon which we all reside.

In fact we have arrived at something of a watershed; one where it will no longer be possible to sit on the fence and not commit to a resolution of this age old conflict, one way or another.

Thus, those now fretting about how and where to securely invest their financial savings, just might find that cosmic *Lila* (the Hindu term for the eternal 'play' of the universe) has brought them to an auspicious karmic fork in the road of life. Pointing to the left is a signpost saying "Financial Security" and to the right a sign saying "Voluntary Simplicity." Those whose priority is to preserve their wealth will take the left fork and they will put their money into gold. Those who seek to deepen their awareness and move beyond material dependency will choose the right fork. Those who turn left may find themselves still in familiar territory with no lack of advisers on how to put up barriers against uncertainty and change. However this will merely ensure an extended contract with the dark ways of the old regime. For those who turn right will be a challenge of a very different nature: how to shift away from old material dependencies and towards a simpler and more harmonious relationship with the non-material values of existence; the universal energies that are held back by materialistic indulgence.

Those who take the 'right' path may wish to consider investing whatever funds they possess (individually or collectively) in some fertile land capable of producing good quality, ecologically sound food, fuel and fibre for their daily needs. In this way, they will take control of their destinies and ultimately achieve independence from the clawing centralised control system which feeds upon the compliant serfdom of its participants.

The more we can free ourselves from this unholy contract, the less power it will have over us and our world, and the more realised we will become in the fulfilment of our deeper needs and creative aspirations. Once the collapsing institutions of the status quo have dragged all that has value into the cauldron of its hastening demise, our survival skills (where we find our next meal, how we generate our energy and where we acquire pure water) will become far more important than the abstract economic theories by which we have previously learned to live. The skills of the land will be at a premium, whereas the skills of money making will become a useless impediment.

We can start right now. We can take our money out of the mainstream banks which fund the oppressive institutions of this planet – and put it instead into ethical investment institutions, local ecological food and farming ventures, local human scale renewable energy initiatives. There are also the thousands of localised land based and artisan ventures now springing up all over the planet. We can, right now, begin to end years of energy sapping compromise and finally put our money where our hearts are. Because when the corporate gods are toppled and the lights go out, we shall need to be prepared.

This preparation process can be the start of a new and positive interaction at the community level. We shall focus on acquiring the basic necessities of life from those who are already operating humane, responsible and environmentally benign enterprises, and not those who are exploiting the last seams of planetary wealth for their personal profit and power.

So to those who think they will find their salvation in precious metals, I would call upon them them to think again. One cannot eat gold.

Reuniting the Spiritual and the Practical

One of the most significant hurdles to our development as 'whole' human beings is our attachment to the false separation made between what is considered 'practical' and what is considered 'spiritual'. It is a dichotomy whose origins can be traced back to the invention of Religion: as a human-made vessel in which to encapsulate the spirit, and as a formal statement of belief in one faith or another faith, one temple or another temple, one god or another god, or many gods, or many aspects of one divine presence. In other words, to that point in history when our nature and spirit-led celebrations of the miracle of life were superseded by the intellectualisation and compartmentalisation of such experiences under the specific control of an authoritative body: i.e. a priesthood attached to a church.

Tragically, this false compartmentalisation of the spiritual has played a key role in keeping humankind locked away from the universality of spirit which is our birth right and true potential. So much so that for the past two millennia it has been possible to stir up crusading wars in the name of all-powerful sectarian gods and the blind faith which devotees hold in them. Millions have been, and continue to be, murdered in the name of the leading religions of our era. For those who see themselves as free from 'religious' persuasions, money and power provide the latest totem of worship, but in truth this totem is followed with all the same blind belief as that to be found in fundamentalist religious cults.

When we are mere babies, those of us who were born into the Christian faith are initiated into the protective institutional arms of the church by the ritual known as 'baptism'. Here, the mark of the cross is symbolically drawn on our innocent foreheads by the priest whose finger is first dipped in sacred water deemed to form a direct link to John the Baptist's initiation of Jesus Christ in the waters of the river Jordan some 2,000 years ago. In the eyes of the church – we are then one of its children. This condition can later be endorsed by participation in the Christian confirmation ceremony of our early teens.

All this, of course, is supposed to provide a kind of insurance policy against falling prey to the forces of evil, against the powers of darkness enslaving our souls to the doctrine of the 'Devil'. However, the net effect of taking out this insurance policy (by our parents initially) is to be signed up to a definition of life which gives little room for free thinking or exploration of what 'the spirit' really is or what it has in mind for us. Religion and the church having already defined the scope of our spirit for us, so that all we are supposed to do is dutifully follow the script.

Millions take this road through life, as can be witnessed in the 'bible belt' area of the US and amongst devout individuals and communities throughout the world. So strong are the allegiances formed around 'religious beliefs' that when any two or more clash the inevitable result is conflict which all too soon leads to out and out war. Just witness the current vilification of Islam (and by extension Iran) by the Judaeo-Christian warmongers of Washington who use such vilification to incite hatred, which in turn provides a useful alibi for establishing acts of military aggression.

Therefore, it is very important to recognise how religion and spirituality are often confused with one another. While there can certainly be cross-over between the religious and the spiritual, the reality is that one is a dogma and the other a universal force which can be tapped by all of humanity and which is free of dogma. The big question is: how to refocus human attention on the true manifestation of the great spiritual force which has the power to transform our daily lives and to counteract the forces of oppression that keep a great part of the community of man in a state of somnolent slavery?

Many adherents of the various 'spiritual paths' on offer in today's world seem to feel that it is not their place to get involved in taking direct action on behalf of this Great Spirit. In fact, they misguidedly see activism as contradictory to maintenance of the spiritual path. Many appear to feel exempted from having to take action to ameliorate the wrongs perpetrated against our physical, mental and political world. This is a great error of judgement in my view. While personal spiritual pursuit may cause a bright light to shine in one's own world, it nearly always fails to turn that light onto our oppressors in the physical world. It is because of this failure that our oppressors have largely got away with carrying on unimpeded in their progressive enslavement of mankind and the destruction of the environment which supports all life on earth.

A theory held by many spiritual aspirants is that 'confrontation' produces a negative vibration which detracts from spiritual development and only adds to the negative karma already present in society. However, to campaign actively for political, ecological or material change for the better requires that we confront the reality face to face, in order to know exactly what it is we are up against. Holding a fear that taking such a position might become an impediment to maintaining the peaceful vibratory levels achievable, for example, in deep meditation, provides a false assessment of the truth. In such cases, 'Peace' is wrongly defined as an essentially passive state largely free of any kind of friction. Spirituality thus takes on the appearance of a cosseted precious gem stone or delicate flower, the outward expression of a protective inner world which shuns contact with that which appears to be at odds with its supposed state of inner purity.

Adopting as a philosophy of life such an inward, 'frictionless' approach has the net effect of leaving an open door to those who have no hesitation in exploiting the vacuum thus created. Free rein is given for negative forces to do their worst. At the extreme end these take the form of fascistic, totalitarian oligarchies that hold an almost total dominion in banking, big business, food and farming, health and education, politics, the media, the military and even the church. While such cartels are busy wielding their destructive powers upon our planet and upon our daily lives, those on the supposed path of 'higher awareness' all too often do nothing to work against the imposition of such a regime. By taking no stand, wittingly or unwittingly, they remain complicit in supporting the status quo: a way of life based on aggressive competition, consumerist indoctrination and violence.

This is an innately hypocritical position: to preach peace and yet support violence – the violence that lies at the heart of our psychotic, consumption obsessed, Western capitalist societies. Leaving the forces of corruption unchallenged is simply not possible if one is truly following the spiritual path. On the contrary, a purposeful entry into the spiritual path is achieved through committing to do one's utmost to free our planet from bondage and to protect that which is our Creator's work in all ways possible to us. If this means unmasking and exposing that which is blatantly dishonest, then this is what must be done.

It is my contention that by engaging in the direct defence of our basic freedoms and becoming active in the prevention of our collective enslavement, we discover the true means by which our largely dormant spiritual strength is most fully awakened. This way we become emissaries of a universal higher consciousness and are repaid a thousand times over for our efforts. When the inner work of spiritual practice is coupled to the outer work of activist involvement, we are able to find the balance which once again unites the spiritual and the practical and makes us whole. Both must be entered into fully, for in reality they are two parts of one whole; just as an inhalation of breath is not separate from its exhalation. Why do we need to divide? That is the route of our oppressors.

Inner strength leads to outer action. Outer action leads in turn to more inner strength and so on *ad infinitum*. The resolution to the false state of separation made between these two states is ours for the making. The longer it remains sublimated within one or other of what we call 'spiritual' or what we call 'practical' there will be no respite for our divided world and no resolution to the sickness that holds back planetary rejuvenation.

What we call spiritual is actually the vibrant life force present in all matter, in all life. It is the composite energy expressed by the billions of swirling atoms of which are comprised, all material and non-material objects at all times. At the quantum point of engagement every cell in our body is now recognised as an intelligent being in its own right. This being has all the same intelligent faculties as the individual human being, but in micro-scopic form. The spirit courses through these cells in a manner indiscernible and inseparable from their cellular atomic structure. Everything that exists is at once spirit and material in simultaneity. The material is simply a third density expression of spirit, whereas spirit is simply the fourth, fifth and sixth density expression of the material.

When we humans fully 'come alive' it is said that we can also become invisible. The vibratory rate of our physical body merges with the vibratory rate of universal energy and at that point we are one and indistinct from the cosmic energy from which we once materialised. So, in essence, spirit and material are one and the same. It is only because we have not yet catalysed the true potentiality inherent in us that we fail to recognise the oneness of energy/matter matter/energy and therefore the oneness of spiritual/material material/spiritual.

Once fired up to take the sort of actions necessary to bring radical change into the disharmonious and downright destructive mechanisms of our ailing society, our cellular tissues literally tremble with rising energy. The passion to breathe new life into that which has been callously rendered lifeless raises the spirit (in us) from a largely dormant state to a vibrantly active state. The word 'activist' expresses this condition.

The sense of righteous indignation that burns in us when we are witness to, or the object of, a blatant act of cruelty, deceit or callous indifference, is the spirit rising up (in us) in spontaneous defence of that which is wronged or humiliated. Righteous indignation is a powerful tool in activism. The will to 'right a wrong' is one of the main catalysts to taking action, and it is, I would argue, the natural response for sentient humans. I am not describing the 'vengeance' sought in the case of "an eye for an eye a tooth for a tooth" but the burning pain one feels out of empathy and compassion for a sentient life force which is being subjected to unreasonable exploitation.

This pain is the response of the universal spirit which vibrates through all of us and which grows in strength the more we follow its call. Thus, those who see great wrongs being committed on this planet and respond by taking action to defend and ameliorate that which suffers and thereby to bring the true spirit back to life, are truly following the spiritual road to consciousness, awareness and enlightenment. Their actions are the spontaneous expression of all that is Godly in us. To ignore, suppress or subvert such a response is to deny the free expression of this higher calling. It is more than time for everyone to become an activist.

Financial Collapse and
the Reversion to the Local

Read the daily news, even in a relatively mainstream newspaper, and you cannot fail to notice that an unprecedented event is unfolding in front of our very eyes; the simultaneous collapse of two of the World's largest economies: the US and European Union. Both appear to be teetering at the edge of a financial precipice and the great politico-bureaucratic machines that run the show – on both sides of the Atlantic – seem incapable of agreeing what economic medicine might keep this beast on the rails.

They, and we, are now learning that in a finite world no resource is infinite, least of all institutionalised financial wealth whose very existence is dependent upon interest payments made on capital lent to those who cannot sustain the levels of repayments demanded of them. In a 'debt based' economy (which ours is) all participants will ultimately end up as losers. We cannot know the exact timing surrounding the unhinging of a large sector of the global market place, but that some form of large scale collapse is imminent, there can be little doubt. With this collapse will also ultimately go the entire foundation of modern day capitalism, and particularly the 'perpetual growth' based economic formulae that have driven this planet to the edge of ecocide and the mad growth machine perilously close to its own ultimate demise. The vast debt based financial manipulations of the past decade already signalled that a global crisis was in the making. And attempts to solve this crisis by applying an ever tighter squeeze on the already minimal assets of the working man and woman has now reached a 'back against the wall' point of no return, provoking the first waves of citizen based 'non-compliance' uprisings. We are likely to see more of these as the elite bankers and corporate despots who hold the reins of power try to hang onto this power by exerting their repressive authority on an increasingly disenchanted populace.

The entire edifice of 'modern civilisation' is collapsing in on itself, exposing the myth that it was built on secure and solid foundations. Thus the centuries old profligate 'top down' theft of both people and the planet is now rebounding on its perpetrators, dragging all and sundry in its turbulent wake. As a result we are, in the next half-decade, going to pass through the vortex of a huge change to our customary ways of life. This is a change for the better, if you don't like the 'take-all' consumerist package at the helm of modern neo-liberal capitalism, but a change for the worse if you do.

Desperate rescue attempts will of course take place in which trillions of dollars, euros, pounds, yen and roubles will be thrown at the sinking banks, financial institutions and corporate marketing machines, in a vain attempt to resuscitate – one more time – the dying machine. But it won't rise again because there is no crane big enough to lift it out of the grave it has dug for itself.

What will this mean to you and me? The answer will depend on how reliant we each are on the trappings of this materialistic neo-liberal economy. If we are heavily reliant, we will have a long way to fall and will not have an easy landing. If we are not too trapped we will have less far to fall and may have a softer landing. However, we will all be subjected to an intense propaganda campaign as the wounded beast throws out its grasping tentacles to try to further enslave us in its accelerating demise.

We should beware of this campaign. We shall continue to be heavily indoctrinated not to let go of old patterns of thought and behaviour which give a false sense of security concerning the strength of the status quo to see us through "these hard times". We shall be lent on – even by our friends – to toe the line and submit to the "austerity" measures dictated by our increasingly autocratic governments. Beware of this, for it is a deception. Austerity demands that hard working people continue to cut back on their meagre savings in order to enable the elite wealth mongers to maintain their seemingly impenetrable financial empires.

Crises are created by those at the sharp end of the power pyramid and have proven to be invaluable tools for the enslavement of the many. The main card in their austerity pack is the 'fear card'. If we can be made to feel sufficiently frightened of what may lie on the other side of the collapsing financial world which is their citadel, then we will be more likely to do all that we are asked to do to avoid further rocking the boat. However, this is the road to unconditional slavery – and it's what dying monsters feed upon to retain their self-delusions of power.

So, if we want to avoid serfdom to the beast, we had better sit down and honestly ask ourselves here and now – before it's too late – just what might lie on the other side of global economic collapse?

It will require some fortitude to look this question in the eye. For to do so involves a deepening of our perceptions of what is actually going on around us and a willingness to research what forces stand behind extreme cyclical historical events. It also requires recognition of the part that we ourselves – as well as our ancestors – have played in bringing about such crises and an awareness of the fact that they are largely a reflection of our own state of being. For the road to the great collapse is a long and pothole strewn one and is made up of many decades of blind adherence to false Gods. We are all complicit – on different levels – and only by admitting this can we start to put things right.

When we have crossed this first hurdle, we shall be able to begin constructing a proper platform for positive change. This platform will necessarily reintroduce us to some very simple premises for the steps we must take to avoid being swept away, or reduced to serfdom, by the tsunami of global upheavals that are now under way. I use the term tsunami advisedly because the way the planet has been treated over many generations of abject resource plundering, perpetual war and the toxic poisoning associated with excessive corporate greed, has resulted in a state of unprecedented geological, atmospheric and social destabilisation. That state is mirrored by the current financial meltdown itself. How could it be otherwise? The two are inseparably locked into a cycle of cause and effect that has now reached breaking point.

Our ecology and climate cannot exist in hermetically sealed isolation from our financial activities. The wounds we inflict upon our Earth reverberate throughout the natural world (including human society) and the repercussions return to haunt us. So, in taking our first steps to mitigate (for ourselves and our communities) the effects of a world succumbing to both geological and financial turmoil, some very elementary questions shift into the foreground:

"Will I have the ability to procure enough food to feed myself and my family?"

"How can I be sure to have regular access to this resource?"

"How will we ensure that we have the basic security of a home, fresh water, warm clothes and enough energy to provide warmth, light and adequate cooking facilities?"

"What about other people?"

"What if our savings are not enough to buy what we need?

"What if supplies dry up?"

All these questions will crowd into the mind once we allow ourselves to face the truth. They are very valid questions – and they have answers. However, the right answers will not be arrived at via panic or fear. They must be nurtured into existence through prioritising another medium, an approach to problem solving which draws upon our latent creativity, inventive powers and love of life. As Albert Einstein so aptly pointed out: "One cannot solve an existing problem using the same mode of

122

thinking which created it."

Metaphorically speaking the answer to all our questions lies 'right in our own back yards'. Metaphysically speaking, we shall be guided – provided we remain flexible enough to allow our old skin to fall away and a new skin to emerge in its place. This is the very same process which our planet is now undergoing via the tumultuous cleansing process which will ultimately throw off the toxic burden of generations of misguided inhabitants.

So now is the time to act in mitigation before the collapsing structures of the old regime force us into last minute panic based survival actions. Emerging amongst the detritus of failing financial institutions and the war stained ambitions of global corporate giants is a growing awareness that we have almost completely neglected the resources we have available to us right in front of our eyes. We are becoming aware that a global problem often has a local solution and that this solution need not involve a seemingly inevitable descent into a lowly and disagreeable struggle to survive. On the contrary, it could lead to a more honest and simple approach to life which could enrich, rather than impoverish, the spirit while redeeming a lost sense of connection with the natural world.

Should enough of us decide to pursue such a path now, we just might be able to relieve our planet of a whole extra level of suffering which is sure to be experienced unless a significant change of course is undertaken by a critical mass of humanity. In the final analysis, there is not much choice in this matter. Once a combination of crises in the food, air, energy and water sectors reaches criticality – many are either not going to be able to afford to fulfil their customary daily needs or will not be able to access them due to transport and infrastructural blockages.

However, we are conditioned to believe that such events will probably never actually happen in Western Europe and North America. Our corporate owned western media does not want to unduly alarm paid up members of 'consumer-society plc.' They do not want too many thinking they might have to change their ways – for example by ceasing to watch TV and to stop buying from supermarkets. So, as long as we carry on consuming "the daily diet for the dumbed down" there is little or no chance of responding to the rising winds of change that are blowing across our overburdened planet. But free the mind and take a few steps out of this virtual reality world which we have so carefully constructed for ourselves – and suddenly the truth starts to make itself felt.

And just what is this truth? It was expressed very nicely by Dr E.F. (Fritz) Schumacher, the author of *Small Is Beautiful*, as early as the 1970s. While lecturing in North America, he was asked if a switch from fossil fuels to human scale and regional renewable energy sources would mean that we would all have to accept "a lower standard of living?" "No," he replied "I don't subscribe to the term 'lower standard of living' to describe a state in which we freely elect to move towards a life of voluntary simplicity."

A life of voluntary simplicity means a turning away from the heavy ecological footprint excesses of our twenty-first century consumer society and finding that we can manage well enough – or even rather better – on rather a little; provided that this 'rather a little' is genuinely good quality and doesn't harm our environment, our body or our soul. An aware mind and a light ecological footprint are therefore prerequisites for life both before and after the forthcoming 'crash' and the sooner we can get started on them, the less devastating the repercussions of this crash will be.

Rather than list the thousands of localised self-sustaining group initiatives that are currently emerging in counterpoint to the tottering globalised economy, I prefer to recommend that we act in accordance with what I have called "The Proximity Principle." This principle, to which a chapter in this book is already devoted, is perhaps best understood as a blend of the laws of physics and what was once known as 'common sense'. It instructs us to think and act on the basis that where we reside (hamlet, village, town or city) is the centre of a circle – and what we need (daily necessities) fan out around that centre like spokes from the hub of a bicycle wheel. It says that we should try to access the majority of our daily needs for our physical well-being and nourishment from an area as close as possible to the centre of the circle where we reside. Thus we seek to access our fresh food 'from our own garden', our local independent small grocer, our farmers' market – or perhaps even directly from our nearest ecologically aware farmer.

Large cities present a serious challenge: some highly creative collective 'greening' is about the only practical lifeline available to citizens living in population densities of over 1 million. Very large cities like London access the great majority of their food and energy from abroad and this makes such city dwellers particularly vulnerable to the increasing oscillations of the global market place. For such vast conurbations, the provision of food alone requires an energy intensive and complex coordinated operation which is likely to break down once secure financial backing is no longer guaranteed. Processed foods require a further energy input and long distance transportation yet more.

'Fresh local food' however requires very little energy input and is alive with vital nutrients and vitamins that are lost in transport, packaging and days on neon lit supermarket shelves – all factors contributing to the demise of our planet Earth. And so with energy: start again from your own wood burning stove; passive and photovoltaic solar panels or small wind generator – or link into a community renewable energy scheme. Obtain your firewood from a local timber merchant or farmer/forester.

Make a serious effort to wean yourself off 'the national grid' and the supermarket (hugely consumptive energy footprints) and start supporting the local traders of your community: when the chips are down and the lights go out – it is here where your solution lies and the relationship we build with our local community will define how well we cope down the pathway to 'voluntary simplicity'. It is only at the local level that we can participate in the intimate trading transactions that connect the ecological farmer, forester, blacksmith, baker and transporter. Having money will not be so important when bartering and exchange once again become community led activities. Unless we are connected into the dynamic of this infrastructure, our chances of getting through coming seismic events without too much pain are very small.

By following the Proximity Principle, we shall be guided towards the most elegant economic, ecological and socially constructive solutions concerning the sane management of our daily lives. Such an approach also has the potential to bring about a renaissance of meaningful relationships (personal, social and economic) and cast a fresh light on shared creative endeavour – in the fields, on the streets and in the home. We shall discover that there really are local solutions to global problems.

19

From Immaculate Conception to Genetic Deception

The Christ consciousness with which humanity is endowed, and which took physical form in Jesus Christ some 2,000 years ago, is a revolutionary gift. It has the power to transform, to heal and to penetrate the darkness with light. However, it is a gift which still remains largely sealed away from human consciousness, covered over by the cult of consumption and religious orthodoxy. What this great prophet of 2,000 years past was able to teach and to demonstrate was that such a state of (higher) consciousness 'exists' and has always existed; and that it is freely available to us all, being an incontrovertible part of our very DNA and of every cell and corpuscle of our bodies.

I have chosen to use the expression 'Christ Consciousness' not because it is any more significant than other high prophetic teachings, but because a significant portion of Western society's spiritual inheritance is founded on the words and works of the prophet Jesus Christ. Such teaching has the role of passing on in the earthly plane of existence that which originates in the great cosmic plane of existence, of which we and our planet are an integral part. However it has seldom succeeded in this role, largely because 'religious orthodoxy' has contrived to take control of the spiritual realm, claiming unto itself 'the moral high ground' and giving itself the authority to censor the revolutionary quality of the original message.

Every culture has its shamans, gurus, saints and spiritual masters. Shiva, Buddha, Krishna, Mohamed and Abraham, to name just a few. All their teachings have a common theme: 'mankind is created in the image of God' and the realisation and manifestation of this Godly state is the true goal and purpose of humanity's existence here on earth. They also all state that love and compassion are central attributes of the human condition. That is why I started by saying that we are endowed with a revolutionary gift.

But when this Godly gift is disassociated from its human expression and consigned instead to being the sole attribute of our Creator – then the teachings of Jesus Christ and other great prophets become fundamentally subverted. The revolutionary 'divine soul seed' which we are called upon to nurture into its fullness of being is instead carefully sanitised and locked away from the light.

Having so disposed of our birthright, we seem to feel liberated, as though we have rid ourselves of some odious burden. But all we have succeeded in doing is to wrap ourselves in a state of profound self-deception and call it 'freedom'. In denying the divine inheritance – which is encoded in our genes – we effectively shut off the lines of communication with our Creator and set off down the road of genetic deception. Genetic deception, quite literally meaning: 'an attempt to deceive our genes'.

Within the Divine Creation Plan, *Homo sapiens* has been endowed with the ability to decide its own destiny: we have 'free will'. Thus we humans have evolved into the unique position of being able to reflect on our state of being as well as use our intellectual capacity to reason, compare and take considered action. The fact that we are born in the image of our Creator and yet are endowed with this precious gift of 'free will' (having control over our destinies) gives us a very special responsibility. Put simply, we have a responsibility to nurture our Godly gift into a proper flowering and to direct the fruits of this flowering into the amelioration of our society and natural environment, so that they come to reflect our state of being. But it is precisely here that we face the greatest challenge and greatest danger.

What happens, if, in utilising this gift of free will, we decide that we prefer not to recognise and honour its source? What happens if we find that the intellectual power of the mind, stripped of its birthplace in the soul, appears to be an adequate tool for dealing with our worldly concerns?

What happens if we put love and compassion on the back burner, rationalising that they hamper our competitive instincts, material drives and personal ambitions?

The answer can be found by looking around us and into our history. A wilful mind, divorced from the compassionate soul, runs amok, bequeathing itself special powers and high degrees of self-importance. It becomes interested in splitting the atoms of its origin and irreversibly altering the genetic pool of nature of which it is part. It starts to proclaim its superiority over all other life forms as well as over fellow humans.

It goes to war and murders with cool impunity. It creates abstract ideas, denatured versions of 'progress' and tunnel vision theories and practices. In short, it steers the deluded human 'self' into a blind alley from which the only escape is collapse and dissolution.

This seems to be where a significant portion of humanity finds itself today; in an advanced state of alienation and fragmentation. Divided into a thousand parts and no longer able to see the whole or remember its true identity – who we are. And yet for many, when confronted by the arrival of a new-born baby on our planet, this loss of memory is suddenly reversed. The immediate reaction is to coo at its shining innocence, its wide staring eyes and curious smile. This baby seems to stir our memory – and what we are reminded of is that we are looking at ourselves; witnessing ourselves as an integrated whole – without the fragmentation. We can say of this little being that he or she is indeed an 'immaculate conception'; born in the image of the Creator. At this unguarded moment we are reminded that our own wholeness and innocence is buried somewhere within and is crying to come out. The little spark of genius that stares us in the face – exudes that same spark which we pushed to one side – because it failed to match the pact we made with the status quo: the pact of mediocrity, conformity and godlessness.

All that is wrong with life today starts here. In separating ourselves from ourselves we establish a dangerous, abstract and virtual reality world. A world which quickly becomes recognised as 'the norm' to be upheld as the politically correct mode of behaviour for 'civilised society'. This approach, which seems at times to resemble the clinical state of paranoid schizophrenia, represents the underlying malaise of modern man and post-industrial society in general. In this state of alienation, 'scientists' tinker with the building blocks of life and biochemists attempt to re-engineer the plant and animal kingdom, ultimately foisting their deluded experiments on mankind as a whole thereby turning our world into a vast and chaotic laboratory. Politicians look on and applaud. This is, after all 'scientific advancement' and therefore not only perfectly acceptable – but desirable. And even when it is considered possible that the motives are more aligned with the lust for profit, power and control, the re-engineering of the sacred seed is still given the go-ahead.

Most important political and corporate decisions are made by those suffering from this psychologically impaired and 'alienated' condition. In fact wherever a top-down, corporate led hierarchy holds the reins of power. However, the fact that such hierarchies are allowed to establish such a controlling influence is strong proof of our own complicity and passivity. It is we who give these schizoid individuals such powers, and therefore it is we who must be held responsible for the outcome. It is here where one finds the most conspicuous levels of denial; so many amongst us seem determined to avoid recognising their role in delivering the state of play we find around us.

Those wishing to represent their fellow human beings in high office should of course, in a good working democracy, exhibit a fair degree of wisdom and balance. They should act diligently and responsibly in carrying out actions that affect all citizens within their arena. They should know how to balance head and heart, so as not to be arrogant or domineering in their actions. They should be strong in rejecting that which is harmful to people and the environment – and strong in pursuing and promoting that which encourages goodness and diversity. Above all, they should be seen to 'practice what they preach.' But as we see, the realities of twenty-first century society are very different.

Does this description fit any one you know in the world of politics, big business or even in academia?

What has become of responsible leadership in our time? Why are so many of us willing to turn a blind eye on the abject failings of others and thereby accept the unopposed misrule of our countries? And where is the voice of the church in all this?

It appears that those who seek to fill positions in society which give them access to the levers of State can only get these positions by agreeing to sell their souls to a largely unseen and shadowy ruling cabal. It is this cabal which pulls the strings of the puppet politicians and senators whom we elect, and it is this cabal that sets the 'real' agenda: culminating in their dream of a top down, autocratic 'new world order', In the European context a "United States of Europe".

The conclusion one draws from all this, is that *it is the denial of the divine in man which inevitably leads to* the *corruption and degradation of the human condition* – and therefore of society as a whole.

It is within this setting that nature's seeds are themselves corrupted, as if to symbolise the alienated state of humanity. We see this all too clearly in deteriorating human health, closely aligned with a chemically corrupted and genetically modified food chain, once vigorous human reproductive energy is increasingly becoming devoid of life and is unable to achieve normal patterns of procreation.

When our true reality is denied 'virtual reality' replaces it. Virtual reality becomes the new normal, embracing a world of deception, distortion and alienation. The simple practical values of yesteryear are lost to a whole host of up to the minute cyber distractions; just as the good robust foods that once filled our plates are lost to laboratory inspired mixtures of chemical preservatives, colours and altered genes. In the brave new world of mass food production, even nanotech inventions are on the menu; while real foods have to be irradiated (USA) and rendered inert because they might contain living bacteria. Life itself is thus reduced to a sterile, denatured package, offered up for auction in the sanitised isles of hypermarket shopping malls.

So what about us humans? There are those who foresee gene processing laboratories replacing the mother's womb. Laboratory colour charts allowing parents to select the colour of the eyes and bio-engineering deciding the shape of the mouth and nose; even the desired emotional range could be programmed into the design. Under such a regime 'eugenics' would be put right back onto the map of 'human advancement'. Already male infertility is running high in the United States and growing in Europe. Is it a coincidence that the spread of genetically engineered foods almost exactly matches the rapid rise in human infertility?

While the spark of a higher purpose has briefly illuminated various phases of human evolution, we appear to have failed to nurture this spark into the transformational fire which would bring forth the Godly in us – and keep it there. And yet, 2,000 years ago, an outstanding prophet helped us to understand that Homo sapiens is created in the image of the Supreme Consciousness (God) and that we *have* the potential to realise and manifest this divinity which lies within every one of our 13 billion cells and which is etched into our very DNA. But we chose to downgrade our divinity and to compromise our greatness, preferring the safety of mediocrity to the risks of genius. What price will we have to pay for such cowardice? What price our Faustian pact with the masters of deception?

A great price, yet because Real Life is a sentient, coherent whole and not the fragmented and insentient state that it appears to be, there is always the potential for a positive resolution, even to the worst crisis. Behind the propaganda fuelled veil of Maya (the great illusion), there lies an omnipotent reality which is the source of our divinity and the fecund pool of our creativity. We have only to access this divinity and we will be guided along the path of deeper destiny and beyond the reach of the masters of darkness. But let ourselves be ruled by the false gods who masquerade as the great and the all-knowing – and we will remain locked into a covert pact with the forces of darkness. We will remain slaves to the technocrat financiers, genetic engineers and corporate gangsters, and no sign will there be that we were born in the image of our Creator.

However, should we find the courage to speak out and to challenge these false gods; to challenge those religious proclamations of the church which continue to repress the revolutionary message of the great prophets – then the new dawn will come rushing out to greet us, holding wide its arms in welcoming joy.

Suddenly, as the light pours in, we can see so clearly the falsities that surround us. We can recognise where the truth is spoken and where the words are shrouded in deceit. We can 'see through' the gamesmanship of political figureheads, phoney academics, and false messiahs. A new world of possibilities emerges in front of our eyes and a new sense of self-empowerment rises in our souls. At that moment we can rejoice and set sail on the seas of a higher calling, in the knowledge that the angels are guiding our voyage and that Luciferian guile can no longer win our souls or control our minds.

This time is foretold in testaments of old, through stories of searing light and apocalyptic darkness. Who will now deny that such apocalyptic times are with us? The virus of greed, deceit, ulterior motive and repression has reached epidemic proportions, manifesting as a pandemic on our planet. And no one can stand aside from some level of complicity in the shaping of these events.

Yet 2,000 years ago Jesus proclaimed "The Truth shall set you free". Now the time has come to act on this proclamation and do away with our complicity with all that drags life down. There is but one overriding necessity at hand: to shake off the chains of illusion and cease to hide from the Truth. Now is the time to move forward and upward and to find the courage to confront and to remove those obstacles that are placed in our path. We each have the joyous task of laying the stepping stones that will reach beyond the Fall. *We have* this power – and we owe it to our Creator to act on it: for we are offspring of the divine sparks of Immaculate Conception and not the sterile clones of genetic deception.

20

In the Vortex

It's just a bit unnerving isn't it? I mean, the way we are all trying to hold on to our familiar patterns of existence while all around us the unfamiliar is trying to bust in and show us something else.

Elements splintering off the old order flash past our cognition at accelerating speeds. Bits fly off the orthodox and once apparently fixed dogmas, disappearing into the dark vortex from whence they came. Once sacrosanct molecular DNA models are cracking open to reveal a swirling mass of sub atomic intelligence rising and falling like human breath. Genetic determinism is dimming fast while the fluid genome is in the ascendancy. While our 13 billion human cells, we now understand, are intelligently engaged in a constant two-way dialogue with the outside world; yet, we still think we think by using our brains.

So what's going on?

Well, for one thing, the solar system in which we live, move and exits is traversing the central gravitational plain of the greater universe of which it is a part. A cyclic event, it seems, which comes around only once every 26,000 years, representing the culmination of a great voyage through the cosmos as well as possibly marking a certain stepping stone in human evolution.

So now, as I understand it, our world is passing through the densest part of this universal gravitational field. During this process our 'normal' three-dimensional experience of life will likely undergo a great shaking down; out of which may emerge something altogether slimmer, lighter and better adapted to merge into worlds of fourth, fifth or even sixth-dimensional experience. But only if we are prepared to allow ourselves to freely enter into such an undergoing and don't put up the shutters.

The fact that this process is now speeding up and intensifying may explain why things are getting a bit chaotic here on Earth and why the messages that pulse out from this vortex are becoming ever more frequent and insistent. These messages are calling upon us to listen more willingly to the voice of our intuitions and to reconnect that which has for so long been disconnected; namely – 'head, heart and hand': truly the rightful 'connected' state of existence for us human beings. Then we should also allow a certain dissolving of the overtly intellectual field of expression to which our Western European culture has become so firmly attached; allowing in its place a more subtle and intuitive state to emerge.

There seems to be a call, perhaps directed towards urban humanity in particular, to ease off the computer keyboard and forsake the city pavement for the plough, so as to sculpt a fresh furrow in the field of life, or to hone the eye to the symmetry of nature and heart to the rhythm of the seasons. Here, the call seems to be telling us, lies an enduring and time honoured river of life into which we are being invited to plunge.

But if we persist in maintaining our old resistance and cynicism; if we deny our symbiotic relationship with nature and the voice of our intuition, if we fritter and Twitter away our chance to move on – it may mean another 26,000 year voyage before we once again encounter such an auspicious opportunity – and what sort of planet earth will we find then?

Of course, it is not so easy to let go of that which has, for so long, been a crutch for maintaining what we assume to be our habitual needs and daily patterns of life. But can there be any denying that we need to progressively let go of the mostly useless flotsam and jetsam of twenty-first century consumerist ideologies? In the UK, for example, we surely need to stop claiming that forty thousand more wind turbines need to be erected on what remains of our green and pleasant land in order to further fortify our unchallenged materialistic dependencies.

Our present need is not to ensure that our 'greened' fridges still function, but that we are able to lighten up sufficiently so as to be able to make the pleasurable descent into that place where maybe no fridges are actually needed.

Beyond 'the straight road of progress' lies what the British poet William Blake called the 'crooked road of genius'. Here lies the world of quantum: a place where sub-atomic particles dance, swim and oscillate and where the observer and the observed lose their distinction, their separateness. Getting us out of the rut of twentieth and twenty-first century specialisation, speculation and separation and getting us into a quantum, connected, holistic state of being – that seems to be the right wave to catch as we approach this new tipping point. Separateness is a lie, a great delusion, illusion, destroyer and war monger; the splitter of the atom of unity. Faced by quantum reality, separateness quite miraculously fades away, revealing a cohesive state to be in operation amongst all the component parts of nature, all peoples and all species. For that is the true state of existence. Is or was anything actually ever 'separate' in this universe?

So, as we continue to pass through the vortex of the condensing universal hour glass, all the hard bits that deny fluidity and oneness, must fall away. All the rigidity, in the form of hierarchical political institutions, pyramidal banking systems, stagnant educational concepts, military might, religious dogma and monocultural thought – all these and more are now coming face to face with their own mortality and fallibility.

Obese hierarchical institutions are already beginning to implode in on themselves, causing much turbulence and upheaval here on earth, as they try desperately to cling onto their decaying pedestals of power. But all such misdirected energies, when confronted by unswerving and uncompromising insistence on truth, are destined to be returned to the great cosmic energy pool from where they once emerged. There to be recycled and transformed; the old hard dark bits dissolved, cleansed and healed, rived through with light again and imbued once more with universal love; readied for their return.

That is the sort of thing which is happening at the quantum level – but it is certainly not what one hears or sees on the BBC or equivalent media outlets around the world.

As I understand it, only that which is etched in pure thought, only that which has, boldly or humbly expressed and fought for truth and simplicity: only such as these can pass through into the quantum universe to come. This can come about as the solar system of which we are an inseparable component, passes through the central galactic plain of the greater universe which is itself only a microcosm of ever greater universes beyond.

So let's pass through, dear humanity. Pass on through – and emerge out of the grey mists of the three-dimensional prison in which we are still held captive. Let's be freed – and free ourselves – to move onwards in our spiralling life journeys: journeys that put more and more distance between our higher aspirations and that which tries to forever enslave us with its sterile propaganda machine.

Can we unite all the disparate parts and know this world as One? Of course we can. Even if much of the human race cannot see it this way; preoccupied as so many of us are with making 'progress' along the concrete autobahn that stretches ever onwards towards the chimerical treasure trove of our power hungry, profit driven 'civilisation'. Ah, but this road is cracking and this civilisation is dying, and as more and more fissures appear in the tarmac so ever more determined efforts are being made to cover them over again and to try and prevent us noticing. All subtlety, mystery and symmetry has already been betrayed and buried because of an addiction to that which is called 'progress'. Even the vast overflowing rubbish tips of our super stupid supermarket culture fail to put a brake on the pernicious promotion of 'economic progress'.

But even now, hacked, vandalised and discarded as it is, our planet Earth still resonates. It still shines in the eyes of those who remain intimate with her soils, her stones, her trees, rivers and seas, still gives uplift to the gulls that wheel majestically out over her heaving oceans. Still spins and weaves the rhythms of the seasons.

"Here, now, I am" is her timeless message to any who can or wants to hear.

"Here, now, are we" comes echoing back the response of those of us who care.

While through the valley in between, bent low in the saddle and riding hard, the four horsemen of the apocalypse make their long and arid exit.

How necessary was their intervention to the evolution of *Homo sapiens*?

I do not know. But I do see that that which is wrought in darkness stands face to face and shoulder to shoulder with that which is carved in light, and that the multifarious expressions of nature reflect this great duality. The fierce and the tender are everywhere reflected in the continuous fluctuations – the Yin and Yang of existence. And we who are part of this nature, do we not also embody these enduring traits?

We cannot completely efface the darkness from our souls; it is needed that we might better rejoice in light. We cannot efface the light, for without it we would have no comprehension of anything other than darkness. But we can try to balance on the shimmering tightrope which binds this duality, which beckons the light and the dark to come unto it. We can strive for this state of balance: that which rises up in joy between the forces of attraction and repulsion.

That is a worthy task for us humans to perform in this life – but is it to be found it in any university curriculum? We, who are the sons and daughters, grandsons and granddaughters of the wealth and empire builders of yesteryear, who see our material-istic options fading fast amongst the detritus of convenience and excess, are coming face to face with a bigger destiny. It transcends the mundane shopping malls and supermarket culture of the present day. We are becoming naked as the excesses are seen for what they are. Stripped of all old props and hiding places, we are being offered the chance to become human. The best chance perhaps.

Many of those battered into submission so that Western civilisation, in decades past and still today, might gain its wealth from foreign soils, somehow manage to remain more truly human than most of us. Those who are the offspring and apologists of the empire builders and destroyers of the Native American peoples have a special task before them. That task is surely to kindle that spark of humanity in ourselves which still resonates in the tribes and communities of those we once tossed aside or enslaved so as to rule this kingdom of earth uninterrupted by mundane concerns.

For is it not in the grained hands and lined faces of those bent on survival that, so often, is to be found the truest smile, the biggest heart and the most honest soul? Here maybe is a clue, lost or obscured from view by our intellectual conceits. Fostered as we are by years of culturally self-satisfied state controlled and private schooling, how are we to recognise that the key to something altogether richer and more profound just might lie in the hands of the simple unsullied peasant or in the innocent gaze of a new-born child?

In the childhood of life, before the spark of genius is so recklessly damped down to conform to the agenda of the culturally conditioned masses, nothing seems impossible. Nothing should stand in the way of the nurturing and growth of that little spark of genius, burning so bright and offering spontaneous gifts of insightful perception for no one in particular and for no particular reason. But too many preoccupied elders have not responded. Perhaps out of fear? Preferring instead to express mild amusement or even disdain when challenged by an altogether other quantum of thought, one that just might redeem our collective joy, if allowed to flourish and ultimately to lead, unimpeded by the encumbrances of civilisation.

And so it is that 'civilised' men and women have betrayed their own humanity. They have snuffed out the little candle of genius for fear that it might upset and subvert the blessed status quo behind whose pillars we still try to hide away. Is fear really to be the lynch pin of this crumbling civilisation? Or can we come through and support the flowering of that deeper level of humanity which is as yet unrealised? To allow such to unfold and grow, so that we may finally overcome the beast of our demise and gain a whole new perspective on the reason why we came here in the first place.

As the time lines of history whirl into the one tightening vortex, past and future begin to lose their boundaries and we our earthly baggage. But if we should venture to the 'left luggage' to try to retrieve it, we might perhaps find there a little vessel called 'our soul' with a note on it saying "at your disposal". Laid bare and at our disposal, to guide us through the gathering storm and to give us the courage to stand firm for truth all along the windswept way.

21

Why Hasn't the Revolution Already Happened?

Remember the Old Testament story of Moses trying to free the Children of Israel from the slavery imposed by the Pharaoh? Well, as much as Moses tried to help the Children of Israel break the chains of oppression, they simply didn't want to take the steps necessary to free themselves from bondage. They claimed that they were relatively well housed and fed by the Pharaoh – and even if the daily work was hard, it was preferable to facing the unknown consequences of a long walk in the wilderness as the price to pay for freedom.

Fast forward some 2,000 years. Calls to embrace civil resistance and to depose the tyrants who hold humankind in a state of slavery are largely ignored. Why?

As the tremors of change fill the air and shake the ground with increasing regularity, human reactions seem increasingly polarised. One set of responses is to hunker down, avert the eyes, close the ears and try to pretend that everything's pretty much okay. Another is to express increasing alarm and increasing fear about where it all leads: the "Did you see? Did you read? Did you hear?" syndrome. It is to all our misfortunes that that these two reactions to the current state of play on our planet remain the predominant response.

But there is a third way: to look the situation in the eye, to calmly assess the reality and then to take action to prevent a disaster and/or to set out a solution, remains a minority response. There are three key factors holding back the revolution in consciousness required to radically redress the top-down enslavement of humanity and the destruction of our planetary resource base:

1. Too many people are too comfortable and prefer to believe what the propaganda machine tells them.
2. Too many people are too uncomfortable and remain preoccupied with a basic level of survival.
3. Too many people remain indifferent or afraid and shut themselves away from the potential to change.

The 'too comfortable' are those able to seal themselves hermetically from the plight of our planet, using money as their main insulation material. Within our Western society these people belong not just to the elite 1 per cent but more probably to the 20 per cent who still hold down jobs capable of providing them with above average incomes. They are mostly on the infamous 'keeping up with the neighbours' social ladder which demands constant engagement with image and the appearance of wealth. 'Must haves' for these people include: the new car, the 'high-end' house or apartment, the right clothes, the weed-free garden, the latest TV, iPod, etc., and the right circle of friends who have broadly the same aspirations.

Not so long ago these people were called 'the bourgeoisie' and most looked to their way of life as a salvation from the daily grind of life on the factory or shop floor, or even among the spreading fields of modern farming practices. Some semblance of this bourgeoisie seems still to be manifesting itself. However, it lacks its old self confidence and is now visibly fraying around the edges. Financial insecurity has eaten into the once predictable pathway to 'bettering oneself' and a bourgeois future for the children is costing more and more to set up. In the UK, the 'proper' wedding alone calls for a minimum outlay of at least twelve thousand pounds.

The social climbers have their focus set on the maintenance of a cosmetic and vacuous way of life which, as far as possible, means remaining untouched by the ragged reality of a world on the edge of break-down. They are complicit in deliberately avoiding dealing with the excesses of their 'lifestyle' or confronting the repercussions which these excesses throw up. They coolly disregard the fact that we live on a sentient planet being daily raped of its finite resources specifically to make possible their senseless way of life.

As if living on another planet, those who are 'too uncomfortable' struggle to get by with little or no security as to how they will make ends meet for more than a few days at a time. These people, and they are increasing in number all the time, have already been ejected from a life of reasonable comfort due to the criminal activities of a combination of corporate and government greed.

All across the Western world, those who have worked hard to get a roof over their heads and some reasonable heat and power into their living rooms, are being squeezed out of existence by the relentless rising costs associated with maintaining a home in some reasonable state of comfort. The majority have little or no control over the 'costs' of living, most of which have their origins in unregulated financial markets (including the 'bonus culture') along with military interventions in some distant land. Only a small percentage of such costs are based on a genuine scarcity of resources or elevated costs of production. And of course they are rendered even more problematical when there is also a mortgage to pay off on the home.

As the rate of homelessness continues to rise, so the machinery of state is less and less able to cope. The state has had the means to look after the homeless stolen by the corporate and banking gangsters who stringently avoid paying state taxes by stashing their vast wealth away in off-shore tax havens or by other equally devious means. So it remains for the working man and woman to subsidise the safety net which they themselves are desperately close to needing.

Those who are unable to know where tomorrow's bread and butter are coming from, quite literally lack the energy and means to create radical change – the revolution which surely should have happened by now. The goal of this revolution is to take back the dignity and self-affirmation that would eventually give all those suffering in this way genuine security, hope and solid aspiration to a better life. But with the 'too comfortable' aspiring bourgeoisie turning their backs on all those less well-off, and the super-rich virtually 100 per cent insulated against the dilemmas of all sentient mortals, the incitement for radical change remains effectively anaesthetised.

So this leaves the main change-making work to those of us who are fortunate enough to have somehow escaped, avoided or seen beyond the standard propaganda-fed status quo recipe for life.

How many might fit such a description? It's very hard to say, but let us say around 10 per cent – and of course the situation remains fluid. Virtually every day we learn more about the techniques being used to try and keep us from coming together to take collective control of our destinies.

We now know that most of the food on offer on supermarket shelves is unfit to eat. We know our water supplies are being tampered with; added chlorine and in some cases fluoride, are just two of the more obvious elements. There are also the pesticide residues and nitrates from industrial farming practices to contend with.

We see the toxic 'chem-trails' being laid across our skies almost daily, revealing startling (and explicitly denied) evidence of the Stratospheric Aerosol Geo-engineering operations being carried out as part of an entirely elicit global climate modification programme. We are amazed, when further investigating this activity, to find that it involves spreading minute aluminium nano-particles in the upper atmosphere using unmarked military and sometimes civilian aircraft. Another element involved is barium: both aluminium and barium are toxic and directly inhibit human health as well as causing significant damage to the

natural environment and agricultural production. The hydro-
logical cycle of the planet is being completely disrupted by
aerosol saturation of the atmosphere which is greatly increasing
fungal proliferation and acidity of soils and water. Atmospheric
geoengineering could just turn out to be one of the most
prominent threats to life on earth barring a nuclear catastrophe.

So why is it that climatologists, green organisations, scientists,
media commentators and government officials all deny that this
is happening? 'Climate Change' is an absurd notion when
confined to everyday human made emissions of CO2, methane
and other pollutants associated with modern, urbanised
humanity, and abstracted from wider issues such as the worship
of technology for its own sake (including, often, so-called 'green
technologies'), the 'military-industrial complex' and the current
state of perpetual war.

The deliberate alteration of the world's climate has, it turns
out, been going on for decades and is mostly highly visible to the
naked eye. Its origins and evolution are outlined in US military
documents, but it is applied globally, thus causing massive
disruption to once relatively natural weather cycles.

Military exercises are also coupled with HAARP (High
Frequency Active Auroral Research Program) technologies,
which have their main base in Alaska and transmit intense
electro-magnetic pulses into the ionosphere. The charged ionosphere then acts as a shield to bounce weather altering pulses back
to earth. Therefore, we have interruptive 'human made' weather
technology being applied around the globe, with only a few
people having any comprehension of what is going on.

Climate change is therefore a multi-faceted issue touching
upon almost every aspect of the way we, in the so-called
developed world, are choosing to live and the values we impose
on fellow humans and the natural world. It cannot be addressed
merely by trimming the edges of our civilisation or by attempting
a more 'sustainable' version of our way of life. Instead, we shall

have to question some of our most basic assumptions about development, growth and what constitutes legitimate 'security' and 'defence'. We shall also have to establish a different rhythm of life that is more in keeping with nature's own internal rhythms and this becomes a rediscovery of our true humanity. Any 'campaign against climate change' which does not include a critique of turbo-capitalism and the military-industrial complex is, I fear, doomed to failure – or worse still, being co-opted by those very forces that are denaturing the Earth.

But this is not the end of the story. Turning back to the land again, we find that the thousands of masts which stream the messages to our cell phones (I no longer have one) act as a distribution network for an ever increasing pall of electromagnetic and microwave smog which addles our brains and destabilises our metabolisms. Unpalatable truths like these cannot be ignored. It is not just our own lives that are at risk, but the lives of every one of us who share this unique living space: our planet Earth.

So it is that we come to recognise more and more how 'the system', which we are largely complicit in allowing to take a controlling influence over our lives, tries to impose a state of technological dictatorship, spreading fear and upheaval so that many ultimately succumb to 'shock created acquiescence' and seek 'protection' from whoever might seem to be offering it. And we note that it is the despotic corporate elite who most generously offer such protection. A protection that accords with the particular priorities of their nefarious aspirations such as: the establishment of a global banking cartel acquiring absolute power and moving the world economy towards dependence upon a single currency; national political institutions being ejected and replaced by a fascistic regime of global governance. This regime then taking upon itself the power to set unimpeded autocratic policies that place food production, energy, medicine, the military and education into the hands of an all powerful oligarchy.

Yes, we are now close, perhaps very close, to recognising the true scale of the tyranny that is being imposed upon our planet. And at this point we wonder how far there still is to go before the tipping point is reached and the psychotic empire builders are no longer able to maintain their hypnotic control over the majority of humanity, and their brainwashed subjects are no longer able to pretend that "it's all going to be okay."

Trying to put a date on such a key turning point is a pointless pursuit. It has an elusive way of never conforming to cosmological interpretation or to human-made prediction. Our only way forward is to treat each barrier presented to us as a fresh challenge to our own inner strength and sense of purpose. In other words, we should see each closed door as a door that needs prising open, just as we see each crazed imposition as just another sterile attempt to lock us into the cage of fear. Then we also need to be prepared for the worst: a near total collapse of the money supply, the grid and the food distribution system.

We cannot be amongst 'the pretenders' who imagine that such an event could never happen. It's more than possible that it will, and we will need to be able to demonstrate leadership if and when it does. For city dwellers, this means:

- Selling the apartment/house and getting out of the city *now*;
- Finding some fertile ground and learning to grow food, harvest rainwater and utilise renewable energy resources;
- Teaming up with friends who already have access to such resources and are willing to share them.

This is all part of the bigger change which must happen anyway; however when it takes the form described above, it becomes a revolution by necessity, not by choice.

If it isn't a top-down induced collapse, then it may well be a weather-induced crisis, or indeed a combination of the two. The stratospheric aerosol geoengineering process I have already described is playing havoc with the planet's inherent self-correcting capacities and is most probably playing a significant part in species extinction rates which are now running at between 1,000 to 10,000 times natural variability.

Whatever it is that is being thrown at us – and however extreme, our response will always demand courage. With this courage comes a rising confidence in our ability to overcome that which impedes us and then to join forces with others who are on the same journey. It's a journey to free our world from those who cannot, or will not, recognise planet Earth for the jewel it is; but instead only see it, and us, as an asset to be viciously exploited until nothing of value remains.

Onward and upward! We are on a march which must end in victory and it is a great road to travel. By the time our hour comes, we will be lighter, brighter and more alive than we ever were before the forces of darkness imposed their sterile, toxic agenda upon our winding evolutionary path. As the poet William Blake wrote some two hundred years ago: "Improvements make straight roads, but the crooked roads without improvement, are the roads of genius" We only need to remind ourselves that we were born to travel this road of genius and we don't intend to get off it.

22

The Illusory Pleasures of Slavery

This is a little dialogue that I hope may raise a smile. It's about you, me and lots of others besides. I hope it tickles the soul.

IV It's time to give up your present job.
AN No, not yet.
IV It's time to give up your present job.
AN I told you – not yet.
IV It's time to give up your present job.
AN Hell! Yes, it's true.
IV It's time to follow your heart.
AN Oh really?
IV Yes, truly.
AN My heart tells me to take it easy, enjoy what I have, make the best of things.
IV That's not your heart.
AN Oh? Well what is it?
IV Your mind.
AN OK, my mind ...
IV Your mind tells you that you like the convenience of your present pattern of life.
AN Funny, I thought it was my heart telling me that ...
IV Try thinking with your heart.
AN Listen, I don't have time for your clever talk.
IV What do you have time for?
AN Actually I don't have time for anything other than what I am doing at the moment
IV What are you doing at the moment?
AN Arguing with you ...
IV Is that a productive activity?

AN I guess not ...

After an extended pause:

IV You agreed that it's time to give up your present job.
AN Did I?
IV You did.
AN So I did.
IV So do it.
AN Heh! Just a minute! What's the big rush - what am I going to do instead?
IV Listen to your heart.
AN Listening to my heart won't pay the bills!
IV Then ask your heart what will ...
AN Ha, ha! There you go again with your clever words ...
IV Ask your heart where it wants to take you.
AN OK, OK, let's indulge in a little fantasy like that shall we?
IV The fantasy is what you are experiencing in your present office job.
AN Damn!
IV The fantasy is imagining that you are happy to go on this way.
AN Very clever! Now look – I have to concentrate to complete this urgent order.
IV It is another order altogether that you need to concentrate upon.
AN And what is that pray?
IV An order that your heart wishes to pass to you.
AN Oh, how very good of it...
IV You know it's true.
AN All right, yes, I know it's true – and I will change my job – but not now!
IV Now is always the best time to do what must be done.
AN Yes, but right now I need a cup of coffee ...

IV A cup of coffee will not help you. Craving is the root of suffering.

AN That may be – but I want a coffee anyway.

IV Who is the 'I' who wants a coffee?

AN Hmmm ... Well I guess it's the I that I believe I am ...

IV Who is the 'you' you believe you are?

AN That's too philosophical – I have urgent work and I'm constantly interrupted!

IV Who is the 'you' who you believe is constantly being interrupted?

AN It's the me I see when I look in the mirror.

IV That is not the you. You are.

AN Who is it then?

IV The one you see in the mirror is the 'you' you think you are.

AN What's the difference?

IV The difference is that I am the you that you really are.

AN Lovely! I must remember that one – great line!

IV It's not a great line, but it is lovely.

AN You're joking! I'm a wreck! I hate this stupid job - and I'm desperate for a coffee.

IV What a good thing then that it's not the real you who is suffering such torment.

AN No doubt – but just who is it who is suffering this torment?

IV It is the mask that hides the real you ...

AN Go on then ...

IV It is this mask that prevents you seeing the real you in the mirror.

AN Heh! Aren't you suffering too then?

IV Yes.

AN Well there you are!

IV I'm suffering because my job is communication and the line is constantly busy.

AN No, no I hear you all right ...

IV 'Hearing' is not enough – real communication goes two

ways.

AN Then we should talk to each other more often ...

IV Exactly.

AN What should we talk about?

IV How you must give up your job and let me tell you what to do next.

AN That is heavily dependent on trust.

IV You don't trust me? The real you?

AN Well, it's been a struggle for a long time now, you know ...

IV Now is the time to engage this trust.

AN Now is always the right time ...

IV Good! I think you are getting it.

AN You know – I don't really need a coffee after all – but I still want one.

IV Yes, there is a difference between need and want.

AN That may be – but unfortunately I still want a coffee and that is the dilemma.

IV That is not the dilemma.

AN So what is the dilemma then?

IV The coffee stimulant distracts you from the frustration you feel in your job.

AN Please don't remind me how I loathe this vile job!

IV Then who is going to remind you?

AN From now on I'm going to remind myself without your infuriating interventions.

IV But 'I am' your I am.

AN Oh you are, are you! So, do you want a coffee too?

IV That is not my wish.

AN So what is your wish?

IV To help you be who you are.

AN And coffee doesn't help in that I suppose ...

IV Generally not.

AN Oh, you mean there might be some exceptions?

IV If you were to take a very small amount and before drinking it repeat these words with true intent :"This is to remind me that I must give up my job and find a way of following my heart no matter what obstacles stand in my way."

AN All right: (drinking a small amount of coffee) "I must give up my job and find a way of following my heart no matter what obstacles stand in my way."

At this point the dialogue is interrupted by the irate voice of the department manager "What the hell do you think you're doing? How often have I told you to complete this order on time – and now you have missed the deadline! You're fired!"

After a considerable pause:

AN I've lost my job ...

IV Congratulations. Your act of intent has led to your wish being granted. A significant first step in freeing yourself from the illusory pleasures of slavery.

AN I feel better already!

23

Going Back to Our Roots

In the rush of excitement over both government and corporate moves to back green solutions for tackling climate change, many of the lessons so clearly spelled out by the green movement's founding fathers, including Leopold Kohr and E. F. Schumacher, have been all-too-hastily abandoned by those who should have known better.

Not only should we all be questioning the direction in which the environmental movement has moved over the past decade, but we should be asking why it has failed to come up with a dynamic, localised and 'human-scale' solution to the large-scale and government-backed, corporate agenda that continues to dominate our lives and our landscapes. Instead, there has been a growing level (insidious yet quite perceptible) of largely passive and distinctly slavish 'green' obeisance to central government policies and EU handouts.

Energy issues clearly illustrate this problem. Here, it is plain to see the increasing monopolisation of green issues by market-oriented, profit-driven business enterprises and government institutions whose goals bear no relationship to the ones that inspired the phrase "Small is Beautiful" or the potent spark that title once ignited in our imaginations. These market oriented schemes bear no relationship to the deeper concepts of 'sustainability' and 'scale' which directly connect appropriate technological advances with community regeneration and a due sense of proportion in all things.

What we have seen instead is widespread failure amongst large segments of society to recognise that most negative environmental impacts come about because of the profligate material expectations that continue to dominate our Western world – expectations that are raised and continuously promoted by powerful corporate, government and media vested interests.

Government calls to move towards renewable energy resources in order to "satisfy UK needs" (while meeting binding international CO_2 emission-reduction obligations) are really calls to continue to massage the needs of a consumer-fixated society rather than to address any of our genuine needs, which, in truth, remain largely unknown. What *is* known however, is that sentient human beings embody a greater need for spiritual, intellectual and emotional development than for the trappings of material opulence.

The reason why this never gets mentioned is that we have allowed ourselves to be subjects of societal indoctrination, an indoctrination that promotes excessive consumerism as a barometer of human happiness and as being essential for the continuation of the now infamous holy grail: 'economic growth' and ever bigger profits for the dominant corporations.

But the long-sustained myth about the benefits to be accrued by this unending expansion of consumer-driven growth has recently been dealt a severe blow. There is no shortage of evidence of growing destruction to natural habitats and both ecological and human degradation continuing to be manifest even in 'developed' countries boasting a high GDP. Why then, in this 'developed' world, are the majority of green thinkers not converging on finding common and enduring answers to the ever deepening crisis right in our midst? Are these deeper issues being sacrificed to the chimerical imperatives of climate change?

If so, we need to recognise the fact and address it. Countries attempting to comply with national climate-change targets do so by postulating the need for so many million gigawatts of processed energy to fulfil 'x' perceived national demand. However, such calculations are predicated upon the wrong model: the current 'living beyond our means' one. The one that leads to the statement that we would need five more Planet

Earths in order to supply the whole world with the standards of living "enjoyed" by Western Europeans and North Americans.

But what sort of standard of living are we enjoying when, for example, 10,000 tons of food is thrown out of households and supermarkets in England and Wales every day? When every rubbish tip is filled to bursting with packaging materials? When our impoverished soils are still being soused with thousands of tons of toxic agrichemicals every year? When almost everything we purchase today has three or four times less life-expectation than during the Victorian era? Is this still all going to be fine just so long as the generated energy that makes it possible is coming from renewable sources rather than fossil fuels?

The Green Party of England and Wales, for instance, is now publicly calling for help in the development of "Large-scale wind and tidal energy schemes" involving "massive investments" that will "raise wind energy production to the levels of Denmark by 2020". Such ambitions seem to indicate that the Green Party is being swept along by the dictates of mainstream capitalist 'business as usual', in which broadly centralised energy-distribution patterns are maintained and under the same greed motivated corporate ownership – but driven by renewables instead of by fossil fuels.

Some may dispute this, but the overall impression being given is that there is a supposed 'plus' brought about by providing extra jobs through encouraging such schemes, and that this overrides the highly questionable stand-alone merit of the schemes themselves. There is clearly a crisis of imagination in proposing such a lopsided way forward. So we need to ask ourselves: what would a renaissance of genuinely 'people-led' regional regenerative initiatives actually look like?

Firstly, it would reveal that we don't need 'massive investment' in any grand schemes. On the contrary, we need lots of small investments in highly diversified local and regional schemes, owned and run by the communities they serve.

Integrated, local regeneration and 'people-led' creative solutions are, I would suggest, the imperative of our time. There are signs of the emergence of such schemes within localised food and farming initiatives and through such initiatives as the Transition Town energy descent models. However, good as these are, they still fail to touch the broad swathe of green supporters needed to create a critical mass of public opinion for deeper change.

Fritz Schumacher and Leopold Kohr argued most cogently for "appropriate scale" in all things constructed to meet our daily needs; ones that are at once low impact and affordable and make use of local materials, thereby exerting a largely benign influence on our environment. Their words resonate ever more clearly as each year passes. We need to remind ourselves of this and act on such fundamental wisdom while we still have the chance. Large-scale wind farms, vast banks of photovoltaic panels, giant hydro-electric schemes are not the solution in the great majority of cases – not to climate change, nor to human change. Schumacher, in his wisdom, once stated that no structure should ever be built to a height taller than the tallest tree in the area, thereby never dominating nature or humans.

How far we still are from this level of sensibility and vision! Instead we see green energy proponents applauding the establishment of regimented rows of 30 to 80-metre-high wind turbines that are increasingly marching across the landscape of the Western world, starkly symbolising continued obeisance to the gods of mass-produced power distributed through vast, centralised grid systems. It is a startlingly cogent reminder of just how sidelined and ignored the whole issue of scale, proportionality and environmental impact has been in the blinkered rush for idealistically flawed 'green' manufactured energy. 'Scale' as a humanitarian instinct guided by nature, not by money and power.

So it has to asked, maybe even shouted: Why is it that the broader environmental movement is not promoting this sort of subtle and sensitive approach to our human and environmental needs? Why is so little emphasis given to the need for decentralised, human-scale solutions to the most pressing issues of our time? What has happened to environmentalists, ecologists, greens? Have the big environmental lobby organisations sold out to the 'green' corporate lobby? Are they now simply the comfortable purveyors of a superficial and greening of 'business as usual'?

There is a pressing, urgent need to focus attention on the truly human-scale solutions that our world so profoundly needs and not to become obsessed with the grand technological fixes that are being mooted as potential deterrents to a continuously fluctuating assessment of climate change. Let's not be taken in by talk of a new 'Green Industrial Revolution' which so excites political figureheads and industrialists today. We citizens should have none of this. It's more than time to take control over our destinies and cease supporting the out-of-control corporate theft of our futures.

Within the great shake-up which is now underway throughout a wide arena of planetary concerns, we currently have a one-in-a-million chance to do something genuinely radical: to help people take control of their lives at the local and regional levels, within communities, and not further appease the already 'past its sell-by-date' consumer-driven status quo. For this to happen, the 'green movement' needs to revisit its fundamental principles, including (and especially) 'Small is Beautiful'.

24

The Essential Counterpoint

Once we have drunk from the bowl of life we need to replenish the bowl we drew from. Once we have become conscious of the underlying problems that stand behind the corrosion of the arteries of our planet, we need to step forward to make a serious contribution to the process of preventing them getting any worse and in helping in the healing process.

Running through all these essays has been a call to all of us, as conscious men and women, and as citizens. It is the call to awaken our largely dormant creative powers to give form to a very real 'resistance': to seize the moment and to embolden ourselves by taking action.

Yet ranged against us are forces well trained in the art of deception that would prefer us never to awaken from this intoxicating state of sleep which pervades our consumerist obsessed era. Such forces feel confident that they can maintain control so long as they are still able to place before us a seductive smorgasbord of never ending superficial commercial distractions. Distractions that only the few are able to see beyond.

In these pages, we have come face to face with some of the most intractable components of that materialistic dream. But equally, we have recognised the deeper values that are their essential counterpoint. Values that if put into effect can turn the tables, sometimes in an instant, and bring to the surface the rich seem of potential that rumbles just underneath.

Now we are penetrating an era of time where that which presently rumbles underneath is due to burst through and announce itself the new heir to the throne. An eruption which is likely to be of such force that anything built on the shifting sands of the purely superficial will be tossed unceremoniously aside.

Such a volcanic outburst can only come from that which has been building up pressure for a long time. That which has been falsely suppressed for so long can no longer be contained, but must burst forth. I like to think of this as 'the rebellion of the spirit'.

'A rebellion of the spirit' goes further than 'a spirit of rebellion'. A rebellion of the spirit is the life force itself refusing to spend another day serving its gruelling sentence behind the bars of unashamed mind numbing mediocrity.

The purpose of this book has been to persuade you to feel exactly the same way. It asks you to cast aside old fears and the illusionary comforts of the darkly beguiling status quo. It arms you to set your spirit free and then to run after it shouting for joy. The hope is that you will feel able to soar with the wind and splash with the rain. It wants you to become who you really are, by breaking the dull patterns of illusion which the architects of modern mind control have indoctrinated in you – in all of us.

Once under way, unseen higher forces will jump to support this great rebellion. It is in their interests too that we unlock the Godly potentials encoded in every one of our thirteen billion cells. We are after all, an extraordinary experiment which our Creator is longing to see come to fruition.

So it doesn't matter if your passion is food, farming, economics, the arts, energy, ecology, politics, physics or just Life. You will, I sincerely hope, be ready to relinquish that which burdens the soul and to feel readied to take on whatever stands in the way of the realisation of a redirected and rejuvenated world.